BORDERING ON AGGRESSION

EVIDENCE OF US MILITARY PREPARATIONS AGAINST CANADA

BY
FLOYD W. RUDMIN

VOYAGEUR PUBLISHING

82 Frontenac Street, Hull, Quebec J8X 1Z5 (816) 778-2946

Voyageur Publishing

Publicist: Elizabeth Jefferson

Editor: Sean Fordyce

82 Frontenac Street, Hull, Quebec J8X 1Z5

(819) 778-2946

Technical production artists: Chris and Viv of *FISHER*, 204 Clarence Street, Ottawa, Ontario K1N 5R1

(613) 789-6199

Cover design concept and photograph: Sean Fordyce

Production Co-ordination: George McKenzie, GEMM Graphics 2022 Kingsgrove Cres., Gloucester, Ontario

(613) 748-6613

Voyageur Publishing would like to acknowledge the assistance of Charles Foster on this and other projects. We thank him for his many contributions.

First Edition May, 1993.

ISBN 0-921842-09-0

Printed in Canada

DEDICATION

To my grandparents, Nikodim Rudminas from Lithuania and Ludwika Kuna from Poland, William Webster from Canada and Florence Olin from the United States. Immigrants to North America and their descendents here have no first rights of ownership, no destinies of claim and conquest. We are privileged to be on this continent and should strive to be peaceful.

ACKNOWLEDGEMENTS

My greatest debt of gratitude goes to the reference librarians at Queen's University's Douglas Library and Documents Library, at the Royal Military College's Massey Library, at the City of Watertown's Flower Memorial Library, at the Potsdam State University College Library and at the Columbia University Library. Without their professional skills and patience in locating materials, research like this would be impossible. I also thank the archivists at the US National Archives and at the Nixon Library. Many article reprints and newsclippings were generously provided by Michael Klare, correspondent for *The Nation*, by the Center for Defense Information in Washington, DC, by the office of Congressman David O'B. Martin and by the Fort Drum Steering Council. I thank Ross Hough of Queen's University's Department of Geography for making the two maps in this volume.

As the focus of my research became more widely known, numerous private individuals came forward with information, leads and sources. I thank them for their concern and courage. Several times in this work, a copy of an article or the recommendation of a reference opened up whole areas for examination. Although I stand as sole author of this book, it is indeed very much a collaborative project of Canadian and US citizens concerned about national integrity and peacefulness.

I also am very indebted to the editors of *Queen's Quarterly*, the Kingston *Whig-Standard Magazine*, *Harper's Magazine*, *This Magazine Peace Magazine*, *Now Magazine* and Voyageur Publishing for their encouragement and care. The topic of this book has long been taboo. Their decisions to publish were welcomed votes of confidence without which I would not have continued. I felt similarly encouraged by the journalism of Mary Walsh of the *Los Angeles Times*, David Pugliese of the *Ottawa Citizen*, Jonathan Salant of the Syracuse *Post - Standard*, Richard Paul of National Public Radio in Washington DC, Richard Starr of CBC Radio in Halifax and Normand Lester of Société Radio Canada, the French language CBC television network in Montreal.

Finally, I would like to thank family, friends and colleagues who reconfirmed for me the importance of standing forth in the public forum with facts and interpretations that governments and "experts" too often prefer be kept secret or confounded.

Floyd Rudmin

TABLE OF CONTENTS

MAP OF NORTH AMERICA

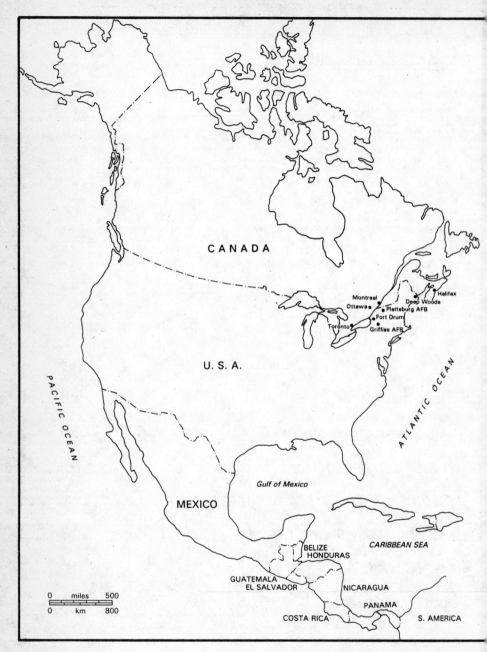

CANADA

Montreal
Ottawa ●
Toronto ●
● Plattsburg AFB
● Fort Drum
Griffies AFB
Deep Woods
Halifax

U.S.A.

PACIFIC OCEAN

ATLANTIC OCEAN

Gulf of Mexico

MEXICO

CARIBBEAN SEA

BELIZE
HONDURAS

GUATEMALA
EL SALVADOR

NICARAGUA

PANAMA

COSTA RICA

S. AMERICA

| 0 | miles | 500 |
| 0 | km | 800 |

MAP OF FORT DRUM REGION

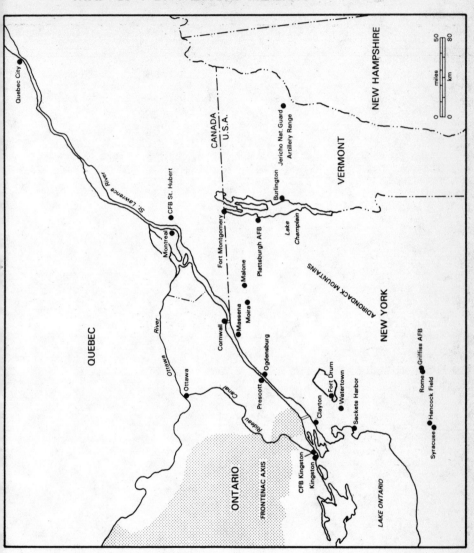

"I say that there is a deliberate conspiracy, by force, by fraud, or by both, to force Canada into the American Union."

Sir John A. MacDonald, 1891.

INTRODUCTION

Fort Drum is a US Army base near the Canadian border just south of Ottawa. In 1985, it became the permanent base for the élite 10th Infantry Division and the reserve 50th Armored Division for a total command of 30,000 troops. This book reviews the history and development of Fort Drum, questions the rationale for the massive expansion there and raises the disturbing possibility that the United States is again preparing for military contingencies against Canada. This concern arises from five general observations.

First, benign explanations for basing the 10th Division at Fort Drum have too many anomalies to be credible. For example, the new Fort Drum forces are called a mountain division by name but are not alpine troops training for mountain warfare. They are supposedly intended for rapid overseas deployment but do not have suitable air transport facilities. They are supposed to fight in hot climates but train in winter conditions. They are for far-away conflicts but have supply capabilities for only 48 hours. They are for brush-fire wars but lack the sustained fire-power to fight guerrilla forces. They are for interventions but cannot assault defended borders. Fort Drum's expansion was the largest Army construction project since World War II and was given unprecedented advanced budget authorization, but a Presidential commission had just reported in 1983 that the United States had surplus military bases and fifty should be closed. The decision to create new light infantry divisions was made outside usual Pentagon planning procedures. The decision to base one at Fort Drum seems to have been predetermined, even though Fort Drum was the most expensive site with the worst weather. There is nothing straight about Fort Drum other than its road to Canada.

The second reason for concern is the mere fact that the United States has garrisoned an assault division — with special preparation for surprise attacks, winter warfare and urban combat — right at the most strategic and vulnerable point on the Canadian border. By geography and by demographics, Eastern Ontario is Canada's natural breaking point. It was heavily fortified in the nineteenth century for good reason. On a map of North America, a single thumb can cover Ottawa, Montreal and Fort Drum. If the United States ever wished to take Canada by the throat and throttle it without having to beat up on the whole great body, the Fort Drum forces are exactly the right type at exactly the right place.

A third point of concern is that this is all being done at a unique and precarious point in history. On the Canadian side, several decades of constitutional crisis and Quebec separatism are coming to a head. Native peoples speak of counter-separation. Western and Atlantic provinces speak of alienation. The Canadian federal government has been implementing major economic and structural changes opposed by the majority of the population. If ever Canada were ripe for internal strife and dismemberment, this is the time.

On the US side, four decades of obsession with the Soviet Union and communism have come to an end. US foreign policy and military planning are now adrift, seeking new antagonists. The United States has a history and an ideology of economic supremacy and ever-increasing standards of living but now finds itself frustrated by excessive debt, failing productivity and collapsing infrastructure. History has shown that patriotically impassioned nations, with military might but faltering economies, are a great danger to their geographic neighbors.

A fourth observation is that a chorus of spokesmen for the political right in the United States have been calling for the breakup of Canada and annexation of the pieces by the United States. Such people have had direct and indirect influence on the Nixon, Ford, Reagan and Bush administrations and represent political forces that are quite capable of arranging events to secure their vision. Their words are warnings. If they now speak openly and declaim their expectation of a continental United States, it is reasonable to presume that steps toward that goal are being taken. The political right has been designing US politics and policies for decades. It is prudent to presume that they continue to do so.

Finally, a collection of curious reports from recent history suggests that the United States has not been the true friend and neighbour of goodwill that most people have presumed. These reports include: decades of secret planning to attack Canada; research into Quebec separatism by US military intelligence in the 1960s; threats and preparations to invade Quebec during the October Crisis in 1970; talk during the Nixon administration of securing Canadian resources by force if necessary; and the continuing construction of new military bases on the Canadian border at a time when other US military bases are being closed. While each of these alone may seem unimportant, together they suggest an unseen hostile undertow to contemporary United States-Canada relations.

FIRST QUESTIONS

I was first alerted to the Fort Drum developments by a speech that the base's assistant division commander, Sherman Williford, gave in Kingston in the autumn of 1987.[1] He said that the new forces are assault troops training for urban attack and house-to-house combat in winter conditions. He said that they are doing this to prepare for conflicts in the Third World. As anyone who has lived in the Fort Drum region would appreciate, it does not take a military expert to know that the base is not a good place to train for jungles and deserts. Winter extends from October to April, and the region is noted for its severe, local, sometimes unpredicted storms. Where in the Third World might troops prepared for winter, urban assault possibly be used? Few possibilities, if any, come to mind.

Two women, one a US emigrant and the other a Canadian with long residency in the United States, independently told me that they concluded from Williford's speech that Fort Drum was directed at Canada. Subsequently I heard rumours that the West German military attaché in Ottawa was questioning the expansion of Fort Drum, though this was later denied by the persons concerned.[2] I began collecting information and going to library resources. The more one knows about Fort Drum, the more suspicious the base becomes.

That initial research was first published in the Winter 1989 edition of *Queen's Quarterly*.[3] It was reprinted the following spring, in full, by the Kingston *Whig-Standard*.[4] Five months later, *Harper's* magazine

---

[1] B. Hutchison (1987) "Expansion of Fort Drum Benefits Local Economy, Military Commander Says," *Whig-Standard*, Oct. 16, p. 19.
[2] J. Picton (1991) "Is US Base Potential Threat to Canada?" *Toronto Star*, Dec. 1, p. A7.
[3] F.W. Rudmin (1989) "Offensive Light Infantry Forces at Fort Drum, New York: Why Should Canadians Care?" *Queen's Quarterly*, vol. 96 (no. 4), pp. 886-917.
[4] F.W. Rudmin (1990) "Light Infantry at Fort Drum: Why Should Canadians Care?" *Whig-Standard Magazine*, vol. 11 (no. 23), March 24, pp. 4-13.

excerpted a portion of it.[5] In the spring of 1992, a followup paper summarizing the earlier research and presenting new information appeared in *This Magazine*.[6] All of the information and argument in the earlier publications has been incorporated into this present volume, often in greater detail and in conjunction with new information subsequently discovered. However, much more research and reporting remain to be done. Hopefully, this book will lead to the uncovering of further information and will encourage people of goodwill on both sides of the border to carefully examine US military preparations against Canada.

SPEAKING OUT

Although now resident in Canada, I am a US citizen originally from the Fort Drum region. That background seems almost necessary for the concern and questioning raised in this book. My grandfather on my father's side was from Lithuania. The Soviet Union invaded and annexed Lithuania in 1940. That heritage may explain some of my suspicion of large neighbour nations. My mother's family has a long history of movement between Canada and the United States. My great-great-great-grandfather, Asa Webster, served in the Continental Army fighting for the American Revolution but emigrated to Eastern Ontario with his fiancée's family in 1784. My great-grandfather, Cyrus Webster, fought for the Union Army during the American Civil War. My grandfather was born in Carleton Place, near Ottawa, but emigrated to northern New York in 1891. I re-emigrated with my wife back to Canada in 1978.

We have lived in Powell River, British Columbia, on the spectacular "Sunshine Coast" north of Vancouver. We have lived in Outremont, an elegant and staid French community in Montreal. We now live in Kingston, once capital of Canada. Our children are Canadian-born.

---

[5] F.W. Rudmin (1990) "Hudson Bay of Pigs?" *Harper's*, vol. 281 (no. 1683), August, pp. 25-26.
[6] F.W. Rudmin (1992) "Playing Dumb at Fort Drum," *This Magazine*, vol. 25 (no. 7), March, pp. 28-31.

I have come to love Canada as one of the ideal societies of the world. I am indebted to Canada for my professional education and for the high quality of life my family has enjoyed even when our income has been relatively low.

This attachment to Canada does not mean disloyalty to the United States. Just as I am pained by the internal and external threats now tearing at Canada, I am also pained by the decline of democracy in the United States and the destruction of its social fabric. The "kinder, gentler society" of which US President George Bush so frequently spoke is not some imaginary ideal. It is Canada. The United States and Canada are both endangered by the continuing, unchecked militarization of the United States — its economy, its politics, its foreign policy, its very values and morals. If Fort Drum is an external threat to Canada, it is an internal symptom of a grave disease for the United States.

My motivations in writing this book are those of duties of citizenship. Military and strategic analysis is not my career. Having noted US military preparations that seem treacherously directed towards Canada, I am obliged to use my training in fact-finding and inference to bring that concern to public view. If I am correct in my analysis, then I have performed a service for both Canada and the United States. If I am incorrect, then the process of proving me wrong will require some small portion of US military planning to become public and thereby accountable. The weight of risk is on the side of speaking out. Societies train academic scholars for this very purpose, to be "gadflies" on the society and the state. Governments everywhere dislike and often try to suppress intellectual dissidents, but we are necessary if democracy is to survive. It is dangerous to allow military élites and secret bureaucracies to shape foreign policy or to have the only voice in issues of national defence.

14

THE "UNITED STATES"

The idea that the United States has active military contingency plans and forces directed at Canada is unimaginable to most people. Much of this book may seem like something out of a movie script; but then so did the Iran-Contra affair. Indeed, both the Watergate Affair and the coup against Allende in Chile eventually became successful films. However, long before they became news and then movie fiction, they were covert reality, unknown and secret from the American public and their Congressional representatives.

We easily say, "The United States did this," "America thinks that," "Washington wants such and such," and thus presume in our language that the United States is a single rational decision maker — knowable, consistent and therefore trustworthy. It is not. The US government is an immense system of competition for power and control. Special interests, manipulations of policies, deceit, coverups, conspiracy, deniability, disinformation, are all part of US foreign relations and military planning. The US citizens we know — the friends, relatives, business colleagues who respect and admire Canada — are not the ones making the decisions. In strategic planning, the United States does not have friends, only interests. National interests are too often determined in secret and then pursued and secured by any means possible.

Peaceful, developed, democratic nations are not immune or exempt from US designs. Even military allies of the United States must be wary. There is argument and evidence that in the 1970s the United States engaged in covert actions against friendly governments. For example, the CIA reportedly supported neo-Fascist terrorists in Italy.[7] It also appears that the CIA had a role in the terminations of the Whitlam Labour government in Australia[8] and the Kirk/Rowling

---

[7] Anon. (1990) "Report Linking CIA and Neo-Fascists Investigated by Italian Government," *Whig-Standard*, July 23, p. 5.
[8] P. Kelly (1976) *The Unmaking of Gough*, Sydney: Angus and Robertson.

"nuclear-free" government in New Zealand.[9] This record of duplicity, coupled with the even longer history of US manipulation of its Monroe Doctrine neighbours, leaves little room for faith that Canada could be outside the realm of US schemes and plans.

I am presenting the facts as best I can find them in order to argue that Canada must realistically look to its security and its continued existence as a sovereign society. Our defence establishment seems still to be preoccupied with foreign wars and is now very much an arm of the Pentagon. Our political leadership seems to be altogether unconcerned. No one is home to pay attention to real events going on right at the front gate. Canada is a lot to lose but it is also a lot to acquire. There are many ways of losing it. Not all of them are inadvertent and not all finders are friendly.

Floyd Rudmin

Kingston, 1992.

---

[9] O. Wilkes (forthcoming) *The Underside of ANZUS.*

CHAPTER 1

FORT DRUM EXPANSION

EARLY DAYS

According to the unofficial guidebook distributed to Fort Drum personnel,[10] US infantry were first garrisoned in northwest New York in 1809 for the purpose of controlling smuggling between the United States and Canada. During the War of 1812, Sackets Harbor, just to the west of Fort Drum, became the centre of US naval and military activity on the upper St. Lawrence and Lake Ontario. The United States again garrisoned the region in the 1830s and 1840s. This period includes the Canadian rebellions of 1837-1838, often using bases of sanctuary in the United States, and the Oregon Crisis, during which the United States threatened war against Canada in order to assert its claim over British Columbia.[11]

---

[10] Anon. (1988) *10th Mountain Division (L.I.) and Fort Drum: An Unofficial Directory and Guide Published for Fort Drum Newcomers*, South Boston, VI: B. Hunt Enterprises.

[11] F. Merk (1963) *Manifest Destiny and Mission in American History: A Reinterpretation*, New York: Alfred Knopf.

R.C. Stuart (1988) *United States Expansionism and British North America, 1775-1871*, Chapel Hill, NC: University of North Carolina Press. **Footnote continued next page**

Canada's defences included the construction of the Rideau Canal system to secure transportation between Upper and Lower Canada and the construction of Fort Henry to defend the Kingston region. The capital of Canada was moved inland to Ottawa from its exposed position in Kingston on Lake Ontario. Kingston was garrisoned with British forces until 1870.

Following US conquests of Cuba and the Philippines at the turn of the century, the US War Department decided it needed a military maneuvres area in New York.[12] In 1908, 10,000 acres of land were leased from the Greater Watertown Chamber of Commerce for summer maneuvres by 2,000 army regulars and 8,000 militia from the New England states. In 1909, the War Department purchased the land and named it Pine Camp. It came under the management of the military garrison at Madison Barracks in Sackets Harbor and was used for occasional summer maneuvres. The next significant event at the Fort Drum site was a mobilization practice in the summer of 1935. The US Army deployed 36,500 soldiers at Pine Camp for what was then the largest peacetime maneuvres in US history.[13] The Army then purchased 9,000 more acres of land.[14] The 1908 and the 1935 maneuvres are the historical origins of Fort Drum. As will be shown in Chapter 7, both maneuvres and corresponding base expansions were set in secret planning against an unsuspecting Canada during periods of peace and friendly commerce.

With the outbreak of World War II, still another 75,000 acres were purchased, displacing five entire villages and 525 families. Pine Camp became a $20 million training camp for the 4th Armored Division, 5th Armored Division and 45th Infantry Division. After

---

A.K. Weinberg (1958) *Manifest Destiny: A Study of Nationalist Expansionism in American History*, Gloucester, MA: Peter Smith.

[12] Anon. (1988) "Fact Sheet: Fort Drum, New York," supplied by Fort Drum Steering Council, Nov. 14, 1988.

[13] Anon. (1988) *10th Mountain Division (L.I.) and Fort Drum: An Unofficial Directory and Guide Published for Fort Drum Newcomers*, South Boston, VI: B. Hunt Enterprises.

[14] Ibid.

World War II, Pine Camp became a site for the summer training of reserve forces. In 1951, Pine Camp was renamed Camp Drum. In 1974, its status was upgraded to Fort Drum in response to the political efforts of Congressman Robert McEwen (Republican), then ranking member on the House Subcommittee for Military Construction Appropriations.[15] In 1978, Fort Drum was compared with eleven other bases for troops returning from Korea and rejected because of bad weather:

Standing snow averages 24 inches [61 cm]. Despite the snow cover, ground frost penetrations of over 5 feet [152 cm] can occur. The northern New York area, including Fort Drum, receives the least amount of sunshine of any area in the eastern half of the United States.[16]

In 1980, Fort Drum became home for the 76th Engineering Battalion and continued to serve as a summer reserve training camp. That unit was deactivated on June 28, 1985.

AFTER 1984

Congressman McEwen retired in 1980, apparently leaving behind Pentagon commitments for construction at Fort Drum.[17] His successor was David Martin, also Republican, with a strong military background as a former Marine Captain and Vietnam veteran.[18] Like his predecessor, Congressman Martin sat on the House Armed Services Committee. The following account of the decision to locate the 10th Mountain Division at Fort Drum is based on newspaper reports from the local *Watertown Daily Times* and the national *Washington Post*, both supplied by Mr. Martin's office.[19] It seems

---

[15] D.C. Shampine and M.J. Davis (1987) "Two Congressmen, Soldiers Turn Dirt," *Watertown Daily Times*, May 29, pp. 32, 18.

[16] M.S. Sowell (1978) *Environment Impact Statement Concerning the Restationing of Troops Redeploying from Korea.* Mobile, Alabama: US Army Corps of Engineers, pp. 44-45.

[17] D.C. Shampine and M.J. Davis (1987) "Two Congressmen, Soldiers Turn Dirt," *Watertown Daily Times*, May 29, pp. 32, 18.

[18] Anon. (1988) *Who's Who in American Politics: 1987-88* (vol. 1, 45th ed.), Wilmette, IL: Macmillan.

[19] These were sent from Congressman Martin's office on Oct. 4, 1988.

that within the first months of the Reagan administration, Fort Drum had already been identified as a site for expanded military activities, particularly those directed at the military management of civilians:

For Mr. Martin, it really began when he got a call to go to the White House late in 1981, when he was told by President Ronald W. Reagan the decision had been made to send thousands of Haitian refugees to Fort Drum for up to two years of detention.

The congressman showed his unhappiness immediately because there were construction plans for the post: What would happen to them?

Mr. Reagan and Defense Secretary Caspar W. Weinberger assured him that after the refugees left, the construction blueprint for Fort Drum would be back on track.

If Mr. Martin did not make any waves, they said, all the promised construction would proceed, and more besides. No one realized it at the time, but that was the real opening for the 10th Division campaign and a military construction effort that could easily pass $1 billion.[20]

About two years later, in January 1984, Army Chief of Staff John A. Wickham, Jr. asked Congress for funding for two light infantry divisions, one to be created by converting an existing division and one to be created from scratch.[21] Light infantry divisions would be smaller than the regular divisions, 10,000 instead of the usual 15,000 to 18,000 soldiers, but the light divisions would have more "foxhole strength," 3,267 instead of only 2,974 fulltime combat soldiers.[22] They would be equipped for rapid deployment — no tanks, armoured personnel carriers, or heavy artillery — so that an entire division might be moved overseas in four days.[23] Light infantry would be used primarily for low-intensity conflicts in the developing countries of the Third World.

---

[20] A. Emory (1984) "Martin's Persistence, Army Outlook Landed 10th," *Watertown Daily Times*, Dec. 13, p. 10.

[21] R. Halloran (1984) "Army Chiefs, In Senate, Press 1985 Arms Budget," *New York Times*, Feb. 3, p. A11.

D. Middleton (1984) "For US Army, New Kind of Infantry Division," *New York Times*, Feb. 19, p. 9.

[22] T. Velocci (1984) "The New Light Division: Will It Work?" *National Defense*, vol. 69 (no. 402), Nov., pp. 56-60.

[23] R. Halloran (1985) "Light Infantry Divisions Give Army a New Force," *New York Times*, June 6, p. B16.

In testimony to Congress, Army Chief of Staff Wickham argued that light infantry could be inserted into a foreign country as a show of force to provide stability for a government in power or to "snuff out" a crisis before it spread.[24] Iran and Nicaragua come to mind as examples, though the Army's White Paper on light infantry divisions explicitly refers to "the British action in the Falkland Islands, Israeli operations in Lebanon and our recent success in Grenada."[25] Light infantry would be of doubtful use to NATO in a European war because they are not equipped to confront armoured forces, though they might be able to serve in limited support of armoured units.[26]

One US analyst concluded: "US light divisions will exist primarily for limited critical situations in remote corners of the world."[27] They are intended to be something of an "in-between" deployment force, with the rapid deployment and élite qualities of special forces and Rangers, but with the infantry-intensiveness of regular divisions.[28] Light infantry would be most useful in quick, offensive operations against an ill-prepared foe. They are surprise attack specialists, with

[24] R. Halloran (1984) "Army Chiefs, In Senate, Press 1985 Arms Budget," New York Times, Feb. 3, p. A11.
  D. Middleton (1984) "For US Army, New Kind of Infantry Division," New York Times, Feb. 19, p. 9.
[25] Chief of Staff, US Army (1984) White Paper 1984: Light Infantry Divisions, Washington, D.C., p. 1.
[26] M.R. Gordon (1984) "The Charge of the Light Infantry: Army Plans Forces for Third World Conflicts," National Journal, vol. 16, May 19, pp. 968-972.
  M. Leibstone (1985) "The Light Infantry Division: Some Observations," Military Technology, July 5, p. 85.
  R. Halloran (1985) "Light Infantry Divisions Give Army a New Force," New York Times, June 6, p. B16.
  Major P.N. Kafkalas (1986) "The Light Divisions and the Low-Intensity Conflict: Are They Losing Sight of Each Other?" Military Review, vol. 66 (no. 1), pp. 19-27.
  Lieutenant-Colonel R.B. Killbrew (1985) "NATO, Deterrence, and Light Divisions," Military Review, vol. 65 (no. 5), pp. 2-15.
[27] M. Leibstone (1985) "The Light Infantry Division: Some Observations," Military Technology, July 5, p. 85.
[28] M.R. Gordon (1984) "The Charge of the Light Infantry: Army Plans Forces for Third World Conflicts," National Journal, vol. 16, May 19, pp. 968-972.
  M.T. Klare (1984) "Light Infantry Divisions: The 'In-Between' Deployment Force," Nation, Sept. 22, pp. 239-241.
  D. Middleton (1984) "For US Army, New Kind of Infantry Division," New York Times, Feb. 19, p. 9.

"a unique tactical style, the key features of which are *surprise, stealth, shock,* and *offensiveness.*"[29]

In his testimony, Wickham emphasized the ability of light infantry to quickly intervene in foreign civil crises and manage them towards outcomes desired by the United States. The White Paper states that "it is important for all of us to recognize the geostrategic value as well as battlefield utility of the light infantry division concept."[30] In other words, light infantry serve to intimidate foreign nations, their governments and their political opposition.

According to the *Watertown Daily Times*, Congressman Martin "jumped on the testimony as a launching pad to get one of the divisions assigned to Fort Drum as a permanent station."[31] Though a Republican, Martin mustered the support of many New York State Democrats. These supporters included Congressman Samuel Stratton, a high-ranking member of the House Armed Services Committee, Congressman Joseph P. Addabbo, chairman of the House Appropriations Defense Subcommittee, Senator Patrick Moynihan, and Governor Mario Cuomo. Support also came from Republican Senator Alfonse D'Amato and various state legislators and local politicians.[32]

The *Watertown Daily Times* account explained that other states were competing for the new divisions:

A leading competitor for Fort Drum was Fort Benning, Ga., but Mr. Martin moved to gain the help of Georgia members of Congress, obtaining from them a letter to the Pentagon endorsing consideration of a plan to divide the stationing between Forts Drum and Benning ...

---

[29] Major S.R. McMichael (1985) "Proverbs of the Light Infantry," *Military Review*, vol. 65 (no. 9), pp. 22-28, quoting from p.25.

[30] Chief of Staff, US Army (1984) *White Paper 1984: Light Infantry Divisions*, Washington, D.C., p. 2.

[31] A. Emory (1984) "Martin's Persistence, Army Outlook Landed 10th," *Watertown Daily Times*, Dec. 13, p. 10.

[32] Ibid.

M. Weisskopf (1985) "Community Happily Anticipates Army Invasion," *Washington Post*, May 27, p. A3.

Alaska's senior senator, Republican Ted Stevens, chairman of the appropriations sub-committee handling defense funding, wanted a division for his state, but the Army gave him another new light division, the 6th ...

Mr. Martin's confidence that Fort Drum would be chosen grew steadily. Although he would have been willing to accept less than the full division, when Senator Alfonse M. D'Amato, R-NY, at one point seemed willing to settle for just a brigade, Mr. Martin made sure the senator backed the push for everything Fort Drum could get.

Despite nervousness that any news leak could upset Drum's apparent advantage, it held even though the *Army Times* jumped the gun by nearly six weeks with a story that predicted the decision with almost total accuracy.

By that time, however, things were so far along the track they could not be pushed off. Once the two national political conventions had ended and Congress' Labor Day recess was over, it was just a question of days.

On Sept. 11, the Pentagon said Fort Drum was the "preferred alternative" for the 10th Division. On Nov. 20 came the final word.[33]

The *Washington Post*'s account of the decision to base the 10th Mountain Division at Fort Drum is more cynical, beginning with the observation that the United States has 4,000 military facilities, "most of which are costly white elephants."[34] The report continues:

A presidential panel concluded in 1983 that phasing out just 50 "unnecessary and inefficient installations" would save taxpayers $2 billion a year, but it added that "the subject is politically painful to pursue."

At about the same time, the Army was laying the groundwork for Fort Drum. Chief of Staff General John A. Wickham, Jr. approached Congress in January 1984 with plans to form a light infantry division of 10,000 soldiers mobile enough to move quickly to crises abroad.

Nine months later, Fort Drum was chosen as home of the new 10th Mountain Division, despite Army projections of higher development costs there than at competing military installations in Alaska, Washington state, Kentucky, Georgia and California.

The Army reasoned that Fort Drum was the only place large enough to contain the entire division.

With the arrival of the 10th Division, Fort Drum has a command considerably larger than that of previous decades, requiring it to "plan and support mobilization and training of almost 30,000

---

[33] A. Emory (1984) "Martin's Persistence, Army Outlook Landed 10th," *Watertown Daily Times*, Dec. 13, p. 10.
[34] M. Weisskopf (1985) "Community Happily Anticipates Army Invasion," *Washington Post*, May 27, p. A3.

troops, including the 50th Armored Division."[35] Two other reserve divisions that were not incorporated into Fort Drum command will continue to use the base for training. These are New York's 42nd Division and Massachusett's 26th Division.[36] An estimated total of 60,000 part-time soldiers require Fort Drum for annual training exercises. Air National Guard units using Fort Drum's weapons ranges include the 174th Tactical Fighter Wing from Syracuse, New York, the 103rd Tactical Fighter Group from Hartford, Connecticut, the 104th Tactical Fighter Group from Springfield, Massachusetts and the 158th Tactical Fighter Group from Burlington, Vermont.[37] A-10 aircraft are used at Fort Drum for close tactical support of ground troops.[38]

In step with the expanded use of Fort Drum, a massive construction project was initiated. The US Army Corps of Engineers supervised twelve large architectural/engineering firms, spending an estimated $1.2 billion, to repair 300 World War II buildings for temporary use and to create a "new" Fort Drum.[39] The expansion of Fort Drum is unprecedented in many ways: unprecedented as the first new US Army base since World War II,[40] unprecedented as the largest Army construction project[41] and the largest single construction contract since World War II,[42] unprecedented as the first military

---

[35] Anon. (1988) *10th Mountain Division (L.I.) and Fort Drum: An Unofficial Directory and Guide Published for Fort Drum Newcomers,* South Boston, VI: B. Hunt Enterprises, p. 35.

[36] D.C. Shampine (1988) "Drum Visit: It's No Picnic," in supplement *On the March: Fort Drum Expansion Hits Its Stride,* *Watertown Daily Times,* June 15, pp. 18-20.

[37] Anon. (1988) *10th Mountain Division (L.I.) and Fort Drum: An Unofficial Directory and Guide Published for Fort Drum Newcomers,* South Boston, VI: B. Hunt Enterprises.

[38] Hughes, D. (1990) "Army Units Will Train with F-16As at Fort Drum," *Aviation Week and Space Technology,* June 18, p. 46.

[39] Anon. (1988) *10th Mountain Division (L.I.) and Fort Drum: An Unofficial Directory and Guide Published for Fort Drum Newcomers,* South Boston, VI: B. Hunt Enterprises.

[40] D. Martin (1987) *Legislative Update from Congressman Dave Martin: April 13, 1987,* Washington, DC: House of Representatives, p. 1.

[41] D.C. Shampine and M.J. Davis (1987) "Two Congressmen, Soldiers Turn Dirt," *Watertown Daily Times,* May, 29, p. 32.

[42] M.J. Davis (1988) "Cash Registers Ring in Fort Drum," *Watertown Daily Times,* April 17.

construction project to ever get advance Congressional budget authorization. In Congressman Martin's own words:

Congress, through its House and Senate Armed Services and Appropriation Committees, first had to authorize the Army to proceed with its plans and then had to appropriate the funds to carry out the major military construction undertaking. The military construction budget is submitted separately from the overall defense budget. The Committees approved and the full Congress agreed to a precedent — that of giving the Army an advanced three-year authorization and appropriation for Fort Drum — bringing the total authorized and appropriated for the project to slightly more than $1 billion. The "new" Fort Drum will be the first American military base designed and built "from scratch" in nearly a half-century ... The project represents the largest military construction program ever undertaken by the Corps of Engineers.[43]

Fort Drum is now the biggest Army installation in the US northeast.[44]

MOUNTAIN DIVISION FOR CITIES

The 10th Mountain Division was one of three alpine divisions created during World War II.[45] It was activated on July 15, 1943, trained at Camp Hale in Colorado and served with distinction in the Apennine Mountains of Italy. Deactivation came in November 1945. Despite the unit's name and its history, it is not being reactivated now as an alpine division with special equipment and training for climbing, skiing, winter survival and mountain warfare. This discrepancy has even been noted in *Soldier of Fortune* magazine: "The 10th Mountain Division has recently been reactivated, though not as a fully trained mountain division as it was

---

[43] D. Martin (1987) *Legislative Update from Congressman Dave Martin: April 13, 1987*, Washington, DC: House of Representatives, pp. 1-2.

[44] Anon. (1988) "Fact Sheet: Fort Drum, New York," supplied by Fort Drum Steering Council, Nov. 14, 1988.

[45] L. Thompson (1987) "Alpine Elite: The Making of America's 10th Mountain Division," *Soldier of Fortune*, August, pp. 66-68, 71-72.

in World War II."[46] A National Guard battalion in Vermont is the only Army unit training for alpine combat.[47]

Rather, the new light infantry are intended for rapid deployment and assault, with the emphasis on highly trained individuals and small unit tactics.[48] According to the *White Paper* on light infantry, "The Army sees them as élite units. They will be specially trained for night operations and rapid battlefield maneuvres."[49] Fort Drum's unofficial guide book describes the 10th Mountain Division thus:

The 10th Mountain Division is one of the newest light infantry divisions in the active component total force structure. It is an offensively oriented, highly responsive division organized for a wide range of infantry-intensive missions, worldwide.

Division operations will be characterized by flexibility both in tactical deployment and organization for combat. High technology will be used to increase command and control, firepower, navigation, night vision and air and ground mobility. Equipment design will be oriented toward reduced size and weight for reasons of both strategic and tactical mobility.[50]

Fort Drum's Brigadier-General Sherman Williford has said:

The 10th Mountain Division travels without tanks and armored personnel carriers and is intended to face house-to-house fighting or combat in rough terrain where armor would not be used. In conventional fighting, the division would need armored support.[51]

With the placement of the 50th Armored Division under Fort Drum's command, armoured support would be readily available locally.

The first personnel for the new 10th Mountain Division arrived at Fort Drum on Dec. 3, 1984. The unit was officially reactivated on

---

[46] Ibid, p. 72.

[47] Anon. (1985) "Guardsmen Train for Mountain War: National Guard Mountain Battalion Only Unit Trained for Winter Survival and Mountain Warfare," *New York Times*, Feb. 8, p. A18.

[48] Chief of Staff, US Army (1984) *White Paper 1984: Light Infantry Divisions*, Washington, D.C.

[49] M.T. Klare (1984) "Light Infantry Divisions: The 'In-Between' Deployment Force," *Nation*, Sept. 22, p. 239.

[50] Anon. (1988) *10th Mountain Division (L.I.) and Fort Drum: An Unofficial Directory and Guide Published for Fort Drum Newcomers*, South Boston, VI: B. Hunt Enterprises, p. 9.

[51] B. Hutchison (1987) "Expansion of Fort Drum Benefits Local Economy, Military Commander Says," *Whig-Standard*, Oct.16, p. 19.

February 13, 1985, and was fully in place by 1989. The 10th Division consists of six brigades, with a total manpower of just over 10,700.[52] The division is comprised of two active combat brigades, the 1st and 2nd Infantry Brigades, and one reserve combat brigade designated in 1985 to be the 27th Infantry Brigade of the New York National Guard. The division has enough light vehicles to move one battalion and enough Blackhawk helicopters to move another.[53] Division artillery are also brigade size, consisting of three battalions of 105mm howitzers and one battery of 155mm howitzers.

Tactical air support comes from the 109 aircraft of the 10th Aviation Brigade, which is comprised of an assault helicopter battalion for airlifts, a reconnaissance squadron and an attack helicopter battalion for anti-armour, anti-personnel and aerial security capabilities. These will operate primarily from Fort Drum's Wheeler-Sack Army Air Field, which has three paved runways and one non-paved combat assault airstrip, each less than one mile in length.

The 41st Engineering Battalion is also attached to the 10th Division. Division Support Command (DISCOM) comprises another brigade, responsible for supply, transport, maintenance, medical services, etc. The 10th's Chiefs of Staff are divided into division command, intelligence, operations, supply and civilian-military relations.

In addition to the 10th Mountain Division at Fort Drum, four other light infantry divisions were created.[54] The first of these, ready in 1985, was the 7th Division, based at Fort Ord, California, to the south of San Francisco. The 25th Division, based at Schofield Barracks in Hawaii, was ready in 1986. Both of these are converted

[52] This information was provided by the Fort Drum Steering Council, Nov.14, 1988. Other details of the 10th Division came from the *Unofficial Guidebook*.
[53] T. Velocci (1984) "The New Light Division: Will It Work?" *National Defense*, vol. 69 (no. 402), Nov., pp. 56-60.
[54] Rear-Admiral (retired) E.J. Carroll (1987) "Militarization, the Superpowers, and the Third World," presented at conference on *Militarization in the Third World*, Queen's University, Kingston, Ontario, January, 1987.

S.D. Goose (1988) "Low-Intensity Warfare: The Warriors and their Weapons," in M. Klare and P. Kornbluh (eds.), *Low-Intensity Warfare* (pp. 80-111), New York: Pantheon Books.

heavy divisions. The 6th Division, like the 10th, is a new division, organized in March 1986, and, like the 10th, is training in northern conditions. It is based at Fort Wainwright, just outside of Fairbanks, Alaska. The 29th National Guard Division was created in October, 1985, at Fort Belvoir, Virginia, near Washington, D.C. and was at full strength by the end of 1987. Finally, it should be noted that the 9th Division, based at Fort Lewis in the state of Washington, is a lightened if not a light division and also specializes in high-tech weaponry.[55]

---

[55] M.R. Gordon (1984) "The Charge of the Light Infantry: Army Plans Forces for Third World Conflicts," *National Journal*, vol. 16, May 19, pp. 968-972.

CHAPTER 2

THE DESIGN OF LIGHT INFANTRY

MISSION IMPOSSIBLE

The US Army has usually claimed that it needs new light infantry divisions to cope with low-intensity conflicts in the Third World. Low-intensity conflicts have specific political, economic and social objectives which necessarily limit the type and amount of military force that can be deployed.[56] Light infantry are not part of existing US defence commitments and are primarily intended for fighting outside of Europe. Most analysts believe that the probable destinations of these forces are Southwest Asia and Latin America.

---

[56] S.D. Goose (1988) "Low-Intensity Warfare: The Warriors and their Weapons," in M. Klare and P. Kornbluh (eds.), Low-Intensity Warfare (pp. 80-111), New York: Pantheon Books.

M.R. Gordon (1984) "The Charge of the Light Infantry: Army Plans Forces for Third World Conflicts," National Journal, vol. 16, May 19, pp. 968-972.

W.J. Olson (1985) "The Light Force Initiative," Military Review, vol. 65 (no. 6), pp. 2-17.

M.M. Zais (1986) "LIC: Matching Mission and Forces," Military Review, vol. 66 (no. 8), pp. 79-88.

Said an unnamed Pentagon official: "Central America is pretty high up on the list."[57]

The justifications for the new light infantry divisions have been doubted. According to Rear-Admiral (retired) Eugene Carroll, Deputy Director of the Center for Defense Information, "A wide range of criticism has been leveled at the light infantry division by professional military people."[58] Indeed, many within the US defence establishment are puzzled by their creation. Concluded one report:

> But the Army plan has also been controversial within the Pentagon, where it has drawn criticism from senior Defense Department officials. Lawrence J. Korb, assistant Defense secretary for manpower, reserve affairs and logistics, and David S.C. Chu, director of the office of program analysis and evaluation, questioned the plan last winter [1983] in memos to then-deputy Defense secretary W. Paul Thayer. Other civilian Pentagon officials have assailed the light force as unnecessary and ineffective against some projected armoured threats in the Persian Gulf and elsewhere.[59]

Light infantry divisions will probably be too small and too undergunned to face the armies of many Third World nations, particularly such nations as Syria, Iraq, Libya and Vietnam which are equipped with Soviet armour.[60] Because light infantry must be light and compact for quick deployment and high mobility, they lack the sustained firepower necessary for guerrilla warfare.[61] In

---

[57] M.R. Gordon (1984) "The Charge of the Light Infantry: Army Plans Forces for Third World Conflicts," *National Journal*, vol. 16, May 19, p. 971.

[58] Rear-Admiral (retired) E.J. Carroll (1987) "Militarization, the Superpowers, and the Third World," presented at conference on *Militarization in the Third World*, Queen's University, Kingston, Ontario, January, 1987, p. 14.

[59] M.R. Gordon (1984) "The Charge of the Light Infantry: Army Plans Forces for Third World Conflicts," *National Journal*, vol. 16, May 19, p. 968.

[60] Rear-Admiral (retired) E.J. Carroll (1987) "Militarization, the Superpowers, and the Third World."
M.T. Klare (1984) "Light Infantry Divisions: The 'In-Between' Deployment Force," *Nation*, Sept. 22, pp. 239-241.
T. Velocci (1984) "The New Light Division: Will It Work?" *National Defense*, vol. 69 (no. 402), Nov., pp. 56-60.
Captain A.L. Tiffany (1991) "A 'Light' Infantry Division with More for the Fight," *Military Review*, vol. 71, August, pp. 40-55.

[61] Rear-Admiral (retired) E.J. Carroll (1987) "Militarization, the Superpowers, and the Third World."
Colonel R. Paschall (1985) "Low-Intensity Conflict Doctrine: Who Needs It?" *Parameters: Journal of the US Army War College*, vol. 15 (no. 3), pp. 33-45.

addition, light infantry carry only enough supplies to last 48 hours and must be continually resupplied.[62] Wrote one analyst:

Once fighting starts, they would be able to sustain combat operations on their own for two days. Depending on what the bad guy had at his disposal or how quickly he could be reinforced, two days could grow to be a disastrously short time before the US forces would need to be reinforced and resupplied.[63]

Such a state of affairs is incredible, literally, to many who study US military planning and has prompted comments and cartooning that light infantry are "Kleenex divisions: You use them once and throw them away."[64]

Military experts have also criticized light infantry as just another type of airborne unit. Wrote Marvin Leibstone in *Military Technology*:

Unfortunately, airborne units have become increasingly vulnerable to enemy radar and ground-to-air weapons and require terrain and climatic conditions that do not always exist. These experts add that unless the Army examines their alternatives as the new infantry divisions are deployed for training at bases in Alaska and New York state, the utility of the divisions will remain suspect.[65]

As airborne units, the new divisions have further been criticized because of the inadequacy of on-loading facilities, the need to disassemble the light infantry's helicopters, the failure to base light infantry adjacent to suitably large airfields, the lack of adequate transport aircraft, and the unlikelihood that deployment destinations will have airfields sophisticated enough to efficiently receive, unload, and refuel C-141 cargo planes.[66]

Many critics have argued that light infantry are simply not needed. All conceivable rapid deployment scenarios could already have been

[62] W.J. Olson (1985) "The Light Force Initiative," *Military Review*, vol. 65 (no. 6), pp. 2-17.

[63] T. Velocci (1984) "The New Light Division: Will It Work?" *National Defense*, vol. 69 (no. 402), Nov., p. 60.

[64] M. Ganley (1985) "Are Soldiers Headed for 'Hot' Spots Doomed to Train at Frigid Fort Drum?" *Armed Forces Journal International*, vol. 122 (no. 10), p. 80.

M.T. Klare (1984) "Light Infantry Divisions: The 'In-Between' Deployment Force," *Nation*, Sept. 22, pp. 239-241.

[65] M. Leibstone (1985) "The Light Infantry Division: Some Observations," *Military Technology*, July 5, p. 86.

[66] W.J. Olson (1985) "The Light Force Initiative," *Military Review*, vol. 65 (no. 6), pp. 2-17.

managed by traditional US force structure, which includes two airborne divisions, three Marine divisions, three Ranger battalions and an assortment of Special Operations Forces in each of the branches of the armed forces.[67] Various military officials have argued that "no convincing case for four additional light infantry divisions has ever been made."[68] Other typical comments are:

Those sceptical of the new strategy argue that light divisions essentially duplicate the Marines.[69]

Standing forces such as Airborne, Airmobile, and Ranger battalions in the army — not to mention the entire Marine Corps — leave many officials doubtful that more light forces for quick insertions are needed.[70]

Some Pentagon officials doubt additional light forces are needed for Third World contingencies: "If you try to identify the number of places where light forces would be useful and exclude [conflicts involving] Soviet-style surrogate forces, you come to the conclusion that there is no need for additional light forces."[71]

WHERE TO?

Thus, the mission of light infantry remains a question. How will they be used? And more importantly, where might they be used? This question applies particularly to the 10th and 6th Divisions which are training in cold climate conditions. Wrote Michael Ganley in the *Armed Forces Journal International*:

---

[67] M. Ganley (1985) "Are Soldiers Headed for 'Hot' Spots Doomed to Train at Frigid Fort Drum?" *Armed Forces Journal International*, vol. 122 (no. 10), pp. 78, 80, 84.

S.D. Goose (1988) "Low-Intensity Warfare: The Warriors and their Weapons," in M. Klare and P. Kornbluh (eds.), *Low-Intensity Warfare* (pp. 80-111), New York: Pantheon Books.

Lieutenant-Colonel R.B. Killbrew (1985) "NATO, Deterrence, and Light Divisions," *Military Review*, vol. 65 (no. 5), pp. 2-15.

W.J. Olson (1985) "The Light Force Initiative," *Military Review*, vol. 65 (no. 6), pp. 2-17.

[68] M.R. Gordon (1985) "Army's Third World Strike Force Finds a Home — in Alaska of All Cold Places," *National Journal*, vol. 7, April 14, p. 728.

[69] R. Atkinson (1984) "Out for Speed, Army Plans Light Divisions," *Washington Post*, Feb. 16, p. A15.

[70] M. Duffy (1984) "Light Divisions: 'Where's the Beef,'" *Defense Week*, March 19, p. 4.

[71] M.R. Gordon (1984) "The Charge of the Light Infantry: Army Plans Forces for Third World Conflicts," *National Journal*, vol. 16, May 19, p. 971.

Among the more serious questions raised by critics about Fort Drum is that of training. Fort Drum, says a recent Army Corps of Engineers report on the planned new facilities, "is the only Army post in the continental United States closely approximating the weather and terrain of the Northern NATO sector."

Temperatures as low as minus-35 degrees [-37 degrees centigrade] and snowfall from late October to early April "create climatic conditions unsurpassed in the lower 48 states for the conduct of cold weather operations, Arctic survival training, and cold weather testing." The post is located east of Lake Ontario, just short of the US/Canada border and about 75 miles [120 kilometers] north of Syracuse, NY.

Unfortunately, say some high-level critics in the Army, the new 10th Division's main area of potential combat is more than likely to be the hot desert sands of the Middle East or the warmer climes of Latin America, the Pacific, or Asia than in NATO's northern sector. (Marine Corps units are assigned principal responsibility for reinforcing NATO's northern flank, and equipment for them is now being prepositioned there.)

Training Army soldiers in the cold weather clime of upstate New York only to have them sent off to much warmer combat areas is a waste of time, money, and perhaps even lives.[72]

With the 10th and the 6th Divisions based in northern conditions and equipped and trained for winter warfare, it is difficult to imagine in what Third World settings they might be used:

Argued another defense expert: "The Army argues that putting two of the four divisions in a cold climate is good. But almost all of the scenarios they used to talk about were in Central and South America and Africa. The program just does not hang together."[73]

The Army's original analysis of strategic needs called for two light infantry divisions for use in Third World interventions. The 7th Division at Fort Ord in California and the 25th Division in Hawaii both seem well-situated for that mission. However, the three additional light infantry divisions seem unusual and unnecessary for Third World interventions. The 29th is a National Guard force based in the outskirts of the US national capital. It seems poor

[72] M. Ganley (1985) "Are Soldiers Headed for 'Hot' Spots Doomed to Train at Frigid Fort Drum?" Armed Forces Journal International, vol. 122 (no. 10), p. 78.
[73] M.R. Gordon (1985) "Army's Third World Strike Force Finds a Home — in Alaska of All Cold Places." National Journal, vol. 7, April 14, p.731.

planning to rely upon reservists for rapid world-wide deployment.[74] Major L.D. Huddleston has argued that it is contradictory to have reserve light infantry because reservists are "inconsistent with the desired training profile of the division."[75] Part-timers cannot be élite. However, the Army's rationale is to represent in their reserve structure the types of forces maintained in active duty structure.[76]

The most thorough review of light infantry to date concluded that the 10th Division would be used for interventions in Southwest Asia.[77] This region encompasses the Persian Gulf and includes Iraq, Iran, Syria and Turkey, all of which have substantial armoured forces of the very type which light infantry are ill-designed to fight. Resupply for light infantry in that region of the world would also be difficult and uncertain. The riskiness of sending light infantry to the Persian Gulf region for preemptive intervention and deterrence has not gone unnoticed:

A House Armed Services Committee source adds that the Army's light division concept of quickly dropping soldiers into a low-intensity-conflict zone is "just another code word for Southwest Asia, and if you go to Southwest Asia with a bunch of riflemen, then your shit is going right in the Gulf."[78]

Army Secretary John O. Marsh has vigorously denied that the 10th Division's destination is Southwest Asia.[79] Michael Gordon has reported that the 9th Division, not the 10th Division, is responsible for the defence of the Persian Gulf area.[80] Robert Killbrew has cited 1984 USCENTCOM documents stating that the United States'

---

[74] W.J. Olson (1985) "The Light Force Initiative," *Military Review*, vol. 65 (no. 6), pp. 2-17.
[75] Major L.D. Huddleston (1985) "Light Infantry Division: Azimuth Check," *Military Review*, vol. 65 (no. 9), p. 19.
[76] T. Velocci (1984) "The New Light Division: Will It Work?" *National Defense*, vol. 69 (no. 402), Nov., pp. 56-60.
[77] S.D. Goose (1988) "Low-Intensity Warfare: The Warriors and their Weapons," in M. Klare and P. Kornbluh (eds.), *Low-Intensity Warfare* (pp. 80-111), New York: Pantheon Books.
[78] M. Ganley (1985) "Are Soldiers Headed for 'Hot' Spots Doomed to Train at Frigid Fort Drum?" *Armed Forces Journal International*, vol. 122 (no. 10), p. 78.
[79] Ibid., p. 80.
[80] M.R. Gordon (1984) "The Charge of the Light Infantry: Army Plans Forces for Third World Conflicts," *National Journal*, vol. 16, May 19, p. 971.

two airborne divisions are assigned that role.[81] Further support for the argument that Fort Drum's assault brigades are not destined for Middle East conflicts is the fact that they did not participate in the Persian Gulf War. But then, what is their destined target?

Two executive officers from Fort Drum have suggested that the 10th Division is destined for Central American tropical interventions. Brigadier-General Sherman Williford said that "the new 10th Mountain Division is aimed at fast, tough intervention in the kind of rough terrain offered by Third World brush-fire wars."[82] Colonel Gerald King, second in command at Fort Drum, more specifically targeted Central America:

The problem in Honduras, he said, "whether or not there was a problem," indicates that there is a place for the light infantry in the Army.[83]

But Fort Drum's light infantry did not join the 1989 attack on Panama City either.

GET READY, GET SET

It is unusual, to say the least, that forces intended for hot climate conflicts should be garrisoned and trained at a base noted for its winter conditions. Tailored combat preparations are particularly important for light infantry because of their geopolitical functions and very limited logistical infrastructure.[84] This was a part of the original conceptualization for light infantry articulated in the Kupperman Study:

---

[81] Lieutenant-Colonel R.B. Killbrew (1985) "NATO, Deterrence, and Light Divisions," *Military Review*, vol. 65 (no. 5), p. 14.

[82] B. Hutchison (1987) "Expansion of Fort Drum Benefits Local Economy, Military Commander Says," *Whig-Standard*, Oct.16, p. 19.

[83] D.C. Shampine (1988) "The 10th's 'Granddaddy': King Helped to Shape Mountain Division," in supplement, *On the March: Fort Drum Expansion Hits Its Stride, Watertown Daily Times,* June, 15, p. 14.

[84] W.J. Olson (1985) "The Light Force Initiative," *Military Review*, vol. 65 (no. 6), pp. 2-17.

Light infantry brigades would be configured, equipped and trained for operations in specific regional environments and under relatively narrow scenario specifications.[85]

Captain Allen Tiffany, examining established light divisions and their missions, has similarly argued that realistic planning for rapid deployment requires that specific scenarios be targeted:

No one can claim to know exactly where (in what kind of terrain and climate) and exactly whom we will next face in combat. Therefore, no one can claim to know which assets should be made part of the organic ID(L) [infantry division, light]. But if the ID(L)s are to deal with just one scenario that the Army may be required to respond to, the task becomes manageable. Combat ability MUST drive the design of combat units. A specific combat unit must be built from the bottom up, based on a clearly defined, specific contingency situation.[86]

However, the Secretary of the Army has said that the 10th Division has no specific target region.[87] The local Congressman had a pat phrase that Fort Drum provides "great all-weather training" for general purpose interventions.[88] But William Olson, a strategic analyst at the US Army War College, has explicitly warned that light infantry cannot succeed as "all-purpose forces":

The difficulty here is that the development of all-purpose forces can actually degrade effectiveness. As William W. Kaufmann [of the Brookings Institution] notes: "Obviously, some types of units can adapt to new situations more rapidly than others. But all-purpose forces are unlikely to perform well on any given mission. With time, and knowledge of what a specific task is to be, units can be re-equipped and retrained. However, the necessary foreknowledge and time are explicitly precluded by assumptions of short warning ..."[89]

In a more recent analysis, Captain Allen Tiffany has come to the same conclusion:

---

[85] Major P.N. Kafkalas (1986) "The Light Divisions and the Low-Intensity Conflict: Are They Losing Sight of Each Other?" *Military Review*, vol. 66 (no. 1), p. 20.

[86] Captain A.L. Tiffany (1991) "A 'Light' Infantry Division with More for the Fight," *Military Review*, vol. 71, August, pp. 40-55, quoting from pp. 47-48.

[87] M. Ganley (1985) "Are Soldiers Headed for 'Hot' Spots Doomed to Train at Frigid Fort Drum?" *Armed Forces Journal International*, vol. 122 (no. 10), p. 84.

[88] Ibid, p. 80.

J.D. Salant (1991) "The War that Never Was," *Post-Standard* (Syracuse), March 25, p. A4.

[89] W.J. Olson (1985) "The Light Force Initiative," *Military Review*, vol. 65 (no. 6), p. 6.

Unfortunately, this multimission goal for the ID(L) [infantry division, light] has left it vulnerable in almost all situations.[90]

This emphasis on the local combat environment is also necessary because the success of light brigades depends on local field tactics. They do not have the surplus capacities available to general deployment forces. Because light infantry are rapid deployment forces, they will not have the time to re-equip or retrain for new combat environments. It is "contradictory," explains Major Peter Kafkalas in *Military Review*: "It must be concluded that light divisions cannot be considered general purpose forces."[91]

Yet, there the light infantry are at Fort Drum, on the Canadian border, supposedly because they are general purpose forces. There they remain, even as plausible cold-weather war scenarios melt away. No credible account of the strategic rationale for placing and retaining a light division at Fort Drum has ever been given. For what specific regional environment, what narrow intervention scenario, are Fort Drum's light infantry well prepared?

[90] Captain A.L. Tiffany (1991) "A 'Light' Infantry Division with More for the Fight," *Military Review*, vol. 71, August, p. 45.
[91] Major P.N. Kafkalas (1986) "The Light Divisions and the Low-Intensity Conflict: Are They Losing Sight of Each Other?" *Military Review*, vol. 66 (no. 1), p. 26.

CHAPTER 3

WHY A BASE ON THE BORDER?

A closer examination of the criteria for selecting a home base near the Canadian border reveals still more of the contradictions between official explanations and facts.

RAPID DEPLOYMENT. TRY IT

It was emphasized in the 1984 White Paper on light infantry divisions that regular divisions take too long to deploy to trouble spots in various parts of the world. It is important, the Army claims, to be able to demonstrate resolve by quickly placing division strength forces in regions of incipient conflict. To quote from the White Paper:

Their rapid deployability will enable them to arrive in a crisis area before a conflict begins. By demonstrating US resolve and capability, they may well prevent the outbreak of war. This is particularly so where low- to mid-intensity conflict threatens, when their presence could decisively affect the outcome. And because of their strategic mobility, these light infantry divisions will help reassure our friends and allies — and deter our adversaries — even as they go about their normal training activities in the United States or in overseas locations.[92]

Therefore, the light infantry divisions are designed to be deployed in one-third the time, with one-third the airlift sorties and are intended to move one-third faster than conventional units.[93] Essential to the deterrence aspect of light infantry is their ability to arrive in a crisis area before a conflict begins. Said Major-General John Foss of the Infantry Center at Fort Benning, Georgia: "If we deploy in a hurry, maybe we won't have to fight."[94] In fact, however, the deployment conditions for light infantry are quite limited. Observed one analyst:

First, they are not intended to have a forced entry capability. They are meant to go into a host country, probably upon invitation, where their mobility and high "foxhole strength" can be employed to maximum advantage. They are not meant to oppose an armored force.[95]

The new light infantry divisions "are not equipped to land in the middle of a fight."[96] They do not have landing craft or paratroop capabilities nor do they have the fire-power to assault defended borders. Colonel Richard S. Siegfried, a staff officer who has worked on the tactics of light infantry, has emphasized the limitations of light infantry deployment:

... light division will not have the firepower for forced entry or fighting its way into a hostile area. If that was necessary, the 82nd Airborne or a Marine Corps amphibious force would be required.[97]

Wherever light infantry are deployed, they will need a good airport or a good road and the advantage of welcome or surprise. They will be

---

[92] Chief of Staff, US Army (1984) *White Paper 1984: Light Infantry Divisions*, Washington, D.C., p. 1.
[93] Rear-Admiral (retired) E.J. Carroll (1987) "Militarization, the Superpowers, and the Third World," presented at conference on *Militarization in the Third World*, Queen's University, Kingston, Ontario, January, 1987.
   B. Hutchison (1987) "Expansion of Fort Drum Benefits Local Economy, Military Commander Says," *Whig-Standard*, Oct.16, p. 19.
[94] R. Halloran (1985) "Light Infantry Divisions Give Army a New Force," *New York Times*, June 6, p. B16.
[95] T. Velocci (1984) "The New Light Division: Will It Work?" *National Defense*, vol. 69 (no. 402), Nov., p. 58.
[96] Rear-Admiral (retired) E.J. Carroll (1987) "Militarization, the Superpowers, and the Third World," presented at conference on *Militarization in the Third World*, Queen's University, Kingston, Ontario, January, 1987, p. 14.
[97] R. Halloran (1985) "Light Infantry Divisions Give Army a New Force," *New York Times*, June 6, p. B16.

handicapped if not located near the United States or at least near established US military logistics centers.

There is the additional problem, revealed by the Secretary of the Army in Congressional testimony, that the Air Force has lacked the resources to transport light infantry.[98] Even with fifty new Lockheed C5-B transports coming available in 1989, each plane would still need two or three sorties to move a single light division overseas.[99] Looking at the Army's experience with the lightened 9th Division, Michael Gordon reported:

Army officials are now saying that such a division would be as difficult to deploy overseas as standard infantry divisions.[100]

Specifically considering the decision to base the 10th Division at Fort Drum, it would seem that there was little interest in rapid deployment by air transport to Central America, the Persian Gulf, Europe, or anywhere else requiring transoceanic flights. Fort Drum is located between the Great Lakes to the west and the Adirondack Mountains to the east. The region is notorious for its bad weather, particularly its heavy snow storms which would certainly jeopardize rapid deployment from Fort Drum's own airfield. Because of Fort Drum's unique geographical setting, storms are often very local in origin and unpredicted by continental weather patterns.

In any case, even if weather were not a problem, Fort Drum's runways are too short for the large transport planes used for divisional airlifts: "A C-141 can land at the airfield, an Army spokesman at Fort Drum told AFJ [*Armed Forces Journal*], but the plane would have to be nearly empty to take off."[101] The

---

[98] Ibid.

[99] M. Leibstone (1985) "The Light Infantry Division: Some Observations," *Military Technology,* July 5, p. 85.

[100] M.R. Gordon (1984) "The Charge of the Light Infantry: Army Plans Forces for Third World Conflicts," *National Journal,* vol. 16, May 19, p. 969.

[101] M. Ganley (1985) "Are Soldiers Headed for 'Hot' Spots Doomed to Train at Frigid Fort Drum?" *Armed Forces Journal International,* vol. 122 (no. 10), p. 84.

construction of runways at Fort Drum is now complete and there are no plans to extend them. [102]

Thus, airlift deployment of the 10th Division would require driving over public roads to Griffiss Air Force Base, 90 kilometers (55 miles) away at Rome, New York, or to Hancock Field, 120 kilometers (75 miles) away at Syracuse, New York. The difficulties of doing this have been well described in the *Armed Forces Journal International*:

The logistics of moving the division to those airfields in winter could turn into a transportation officer's nightmare, some critics charge. They point to an average annual snowfall at Fort Drum of about 120 inches [3 meters] and suggest that under even the best winter conditions it will take some time to move the division's troops south along icy or snow-covered roads to either airfield. (Just 20 [32 kilometers] miles from Fort Drum, the tiny hamlet of Barnes Corner holds the state record for snowfall, 466.9 inches [11.9 meters] during the winter of 1976-77.)

The 10th Mountain Division will have only enough vehicles on hand to move one battalion to either Griffiss AFB or Hancock Field. The Army says it plans to charter commercial buses to move the rest of the division to the airfields if need be. How many buses it would require to move the division is unclear, however, says an Army spokesman. "But are there enough buses in the state of New York to do the job? The answer is Yes," the spokesman said. [103]

Even if Fort Drum were to get its own airfield big enough for large transport aircraft, or if new short-take-off transoceanic aircraft were to become available, snow removal would still be a continuing and costly problem:

The Army's own analysis of placing the 10th Division at Fort Drum instead of other posts such as Fort Benning, Fort Ord, Fort Campbell or Fort Lewis, notes that Fort Drum's winter weather will "hamper deployment." [104]

---

[102] D. Hughes (1990) "Army Units Will Train with F-16As at Fort Drum," *Aviation Week and Space Technology*, June 18, p. 46.
[103] M. Ganley (1985) "Are Soldiers Headed for 'Hot' Spots Doomed to Train at Frigid Fort Drum?" *Armed Forces Journal International*, vol. 122 (no. 10), p. 84.
[104] Ibid.

These facts and analyses would seem to dismiss any argument that the 10th Division was sent to Fort Drum for rapid deployment to remote Third World crises.

William Olson has emphasized that if the light infantry division (LID) is to function as a rapid deployment force — if that is to be a credible mission — then there must be some strategic decisions directed to that mission:

First is the choice of an appropriate base for the LID in this country. Ideally, such a base should be colocated with an air base capable of handling multiple loadings and a steady flow of C-141s and their cargoes.[105]

Fort Drum's own airfield cannot handle C-141s. Even if the 10th Division could get to Griffiss Air Force Base in time for rapid overseas deployment, the Army's own analysis shows that Griffiss can handle per day only 218 landings and take-offs by C-141 cargo planes. By comparison, McChord Air Force Base, near Fort Lewis, home of the 9th Division, can handle 408 C-141s per day.[106] For a division intended for rapid deployment to Third World countries to be placed at a base which has severe, often unpredictable winter weather and which lacks an adjacent air base is too blatant and serious an inconsistency to be mere oversight.

One ironic example: On March 12, 1992, it was announced with great fanfare that Army Chief of Staff, General Gordon R. Sullivan, would visit Fort Drum.[107] General Sullivan is the highest ranking officer in the US Army. The purpose of the visit was to promote Fort Drum for further expansion. However, a mid-March blizzard, with a foot of new snow and gusting winds, closed Fort Drum.[108] A little paragraph the next day announced:

---

[105] W.J. Olson (1985) "The Light Force Initiative," *Military Review*, vol. 65 (no. 6), p. 13.

[106] M. Ganley (1985) "Are Soldiers Headed for 'Hot' Spots Doomed to Train at Frigid Fort Drum?" *Armed Forces Journal International*, vol. 122 (no. 10), p. 84.

[107] M. Smith (1992) "Task Force to Tout Drum's Potential for Growth to General," *Watertown Daily Times*, March 12.

[108] F.A. Pound (1992) "Worst Snowstorm of Season Buffets North," *Watertown Daily Times*, March 12.

Today's scheduled visit to Fort Drum by US Army Chief of Staff Gen. Gordon R. Sullivan was canceled because of weather Thursday. No new date has been set.[109]

REGIONAL NEED

Part of the explanation for basing the 10th Division at Fort Drum has been to use the base construction and the operating payroll as a boost to the economically depressed region of Jefferson County.[110] Because Fort Drum is "the largest Army construction project since World War II,"[111] with over $1,000,000,000 spent in fiscal year 1987 alone,[112] the economic impact on Jefferson County is beyond question. Because major construction projects were scheduled to continue to the end of 1991, and because annual operating payrolls (military and civilian) were expected to stabilize at $500,000,000 dollars by 1991,[113] the economic impact will continue.[114] The base employs almost 3,000 civilians.[115]

It seems unreasonable, however, to justify the basing of any of the new light infantry divisions on criteria of regional development. Of the competitor states for the new light infantry divisions that have been identified by various sources,[116] it appears that those with the

[109] Anon. (1992) (untitled), *Watertown Daily Times*, March 13.
[110] B. Hutchison (1987) "Expansion of Fort Drum Benefits Local Economy, Military Commander Says," *Whig-Standard*, Oct.16, p. 19.
M. Weisskopf (1985) "Community Happily Anticipates Army Invasion," *Washington Post*, May 27, p. A3.
[111] D.C. Shampine and M.J. Davis (1987) "Two Congressmen, Soldiers Turn Dirt," *Watertown Daily Times*, May, 29, p. 32.
[112] M.J. Davis (1988) "Cash Registers Ring in Fort Drum," *Watertown Daily Times*, April 17.
[113] M.J. Davis (1988) "The Building's Just Begun at Busy 'New' Fort Drum," in supplement, *On the March: Fort Drum Expansion Hits its Stride*, *Watertown Daily Times*, June 15, pp. 1-7.
[114] E.A. Gargan (1984) "Army Selects Fort Drum as Home of New Light Infantry Division," *New York Times*, Sept. 12, pp. A1, B2.
[115] M. Sperling (1992) "A Different Drum," *Army Times*, Jan. 20, pp. 10, 12, 13, 16, 54.
[116] Anon. (1984) "Army Seeks a Fort as Site for a New Infantry Division," *New York Times*, April 5, p. D30.
A. Emory (1984) "Martin's Persistence, Army Outlook Landed 10th," *Watertown Daily Times*, Dec. 13, p. 10.
W.J. Olson (1985) "The Light Force Initiative," *Military Review*, vol. 65 (no. 6), pp. 2-17. **(continued)**

least economic need were the ones to get bases. The following table shows the rankings of the states' per capita incomes in 1980 and 1984, reported in the *Statistical Abstract of the United States 1986*.[117] Alabama and Georgia are both listed because Fort Benning is located right on the state border. Clearly, regional economic need was not a priority in selecting bases for light divisions.

State	Per Capita Income (Ranked 1-50)		Light Infantry Division
	1980	1984	
Alaska	1	1	6th Division
California	3	5	7th Division
New York	10	6	10th Division
Hawaii	12	16	25th Division
Virginia	18	15	29th Division
Washington	9	18	—
Georgia	37	34	—
Alabama	47	46	—
Kentucky	46	41	—
Arkansas	49	48	—

Specifically examining the basing of the 10th Mountain Division at Fort Drum, local regional development is still not a convincing explanation. Fort Drum is located in Jefferson County, right at its juncture with St. Lawrence County and Lewis County. This region was indeed a depressed region of New York, but New York, as noted above, was among the wealthiest of the fifty states and getting

---

T. Velocci (1984) "The New Light Division: Will It Work?" *National Defense*, vol. 69 (no. 402), Nov., pp. 56-60.

M. Weisskopf (1985) "Community Happily Anticipates Army Invasion," *Washington Post*, May 27, p. A3.

[117] Anon. (1986) *Statistical Abstract of the United States: 1986* (US Dept. of Commerce, Bureau of the Census), Washington, DC: US Government Printing Office.

wealthier, moving from the position of 10th highest per capita income in 1980 to 6th highest in 1984.

In 1983, before the Fort Drum expansion, the *County and City Data Book*[118] ranked all 3,137 US counties by household income. Jefferson County ranked 1,713, St. Lawrence County ranked 1,648, and Lewis County 1,365. Thus, while far from affluent, the Fort Drum region was also far from the most impoverished region of the United States. In contrast, for example, Perry County, Alabama, which borders Fort Benning, Georgia, ranked 3,117, placing it among the very poorest counties in the entire United States.

SIZE OF SITE

Another explanation for basing the 10th Mountain Division at Fort Drum was that it was the only place large enough to contain the entire division[119] and to allow space for further expansion:

One of the reasons for basing the new division at Fort Drum in the cold reaches of upstate New York, Army brass say, is because Fort Drum is an already existing post that offers room to train and space to build on. But a host of questions are being raised about the type of training soldiers will receive there, how much it will really cost to build and operate new facilities to house the division and support the mission, and how soon the new division will be ready for combat.[120]

The issues of winter training, high costs, and impaired deployment at Fort Drum have already been discussed. However, the explanation that Fort Drum was chosen because it is large enough to contain the entire 10th Division is inconsistent with the fact that an essential part of the purported political negotiations for the base was that one entire brigade was to have been stationed at Fort

---

[118] Anon. (1983) *County and City Data Book 1983* (US Dept. of Commerce, Bureau of the Census), Washington, DC: US Government Printing Office.

[119] M. Weisskopf (1985) "Community Happily Anticipates Army Invasion," *Washington Post*, May 27, p. A3.

[120] M. Ganley (1985) "Are Soldiers Headed for 'Hot' Spots Doomed to Train at Frigid Fort Drum?" *Armed Forces Journal International*, vol. 122 (no. 10), p. 78.

Benning, Georgia.[121] Even at the time of Congressman Martin's press release announcing the Army's decision, one brigade was to have been stationed at Fort Benning. The opening sentence of Congressman Martin's press release of November 1984, entitled "Rep. Martin Announces Major Fort Drum Expansion," reads:

WATERTOWN — The Department of Defense has selected Fort Drum, Watertown, New York as the home base of one of the Army's new, light infantry divisions, minus one brigade to be stationed at Fort Benning, Georgia, Rep. David O'B. Martin announced today.[122]

With the arrival of the entire 10th Division, Fort Drum has become a very congested facility. Approximately 60,000 part-time soldiers have been using Fort Drum for annual reserve training, including three National Guard divisions: New York's 42nd Division, New Jersey's 50th Armored Division, and Massachusetts' 26th Division.[123] With this type of crowding, the scheduling of Fort Drum's training fields has become very tight. In fact, it was anticipated at the time that some National Guard units might have to shift to winter training, with the expectation of very considerable resistance from Guardsmen and the employers who must give them release time. These concerns about overcrowding have been validated by the Army Auditing Agency, which gave Fort Drum the lowest ranking among US Army bases largely because of overcrowding.[124] It is not clear whether or not the recent cutbacks in Army reservists will alleviate the problem of crowding.[125]

Although the recent expansion of Fort Drum did not entail any increase in its 107,265 acre land base, there is increasing use of

---

[121] A. Emory (1984) "Martin's Persistence, Army Outlook Landed 10th," *Watertown Daily Times*, Dec. 13, p. 10.

[122] Received from Congressman Martin's office, Oct. 4, 1988.

[123] D.C. Shampine (1988) "Drum Visit: It's No Picnic," in supplement *On the March: Fort Drum Expansion Hits Its Stride*, *Watertown Daily Times*, June 15, pp. 18-20.

[124] A. Emory (1991) "Fort Drum Escapes Ax: Panel Votes to Keep it, Despite Low Rating," *Watertown Daily Times*, June 8, p. 28.

[125] E. Schmitt (1992) "Pentagon Seeking 140,000 Reduction in Reserve Forces," *New York Times*, March 27, p. A14.

neighbouring conservation areas for military exercises.[126] Said one local environmentalist: "It is obvious that the Army wants to expand its land base around Drum."[127] New York State's 85,000 acre Fish and Wildlife Management Act Cooperator Area around portions of Fort Drum is at greatest risk.

There have also been instances of Fort Drum forces commandeering portions of the Adirondack Park.[128] This park is unique in that it is protected, not by executive orders, not by legislation, but by the New York State constitution. Use of park land for military maneuvres should require an amendment to the state constitution, which would require a statewide referendum. Also of concern to enviromentalists, and also of doubtful legality, are Fort Drum's toxic chemical dump sites, one of which drains into Pleasant Creek, which empties into the Indian River, which discharges into the St.Lawrence River at Ogdensburg. It is not known how many people are at risk for using this water for drinking, fishing or swimming.[129]

TOO MANY ANOMALIES

The public explanations and justifications for the new light infantry divisions seem weak. Numerous reports and analyses have identified major faults with the concept of light infantry as rapid deployment forces for overseas operations. Because of limitations of firepower, logistics, armour, airlift and suitable deployment conditions, light infantry appear to be inadequate for either Third World interventions or NATO deployment. Here is a sample of expert opinion:

---

[126] G. Fedchak (1989) "Adirondack Park, or Fort Adirondack? The Impact of the Expansion of Fort Drum on the Adirondacks and the Tug Hill Plateau," *Adirondac*, vol. 53 (no. 2), Feb./Mar., pp. 7-10.
[127] Ibid., p. 8.
[128] Ibid.
[129] S. Burtch (1990) "The Drums of Fort Drum," *Between the Lines*, May 24, pp. 10-11.

Unfortunately, the LID is not likely to be adequate to many of the situations for which it is intended. It may be able to deploy quickly, but it may not be able to survive once deployed.[130]

If the light division is used in a conflict, "it won't have enough [men left] to carry the bodies away," says one high-level Army source.[131]

"The idea seems to be to get there so fast you absolutely bedazzle the enemy," said Thomas L. McNaugher, a research associate at the Brookings Institution. "But once you get there you cannot really do anything." [132]

Colonel Dale K. Brudvig, a Pentagon staff officer, agreed that a light division could be moved quickly. But, in an article in *The Army Times*, a weekly newspaper for the Army, he wrote, "The question is: What can the light division fight?" [133]

Many of these same critics have argued that the new light infantry divisions duplicate existing rapid deployment, intervention forces and are therefore simply unnecessary. In the words of a Congressional source following the light infantry debate:

There is a very real growing opinion around here that those units are units looking for an excuse to happen ... They are busy building units that you don't have a rational explanation of what you are going to use them for.[134]

That light infantry are inadequate for overseas missions may indicate incompetent military planning. It may also indicate that military planners have other missions in mind closer to home.

If the explanations and justifications for light infantry generally seem irrational, the basing of the 10th Mountain Division at Fort Drum seems doubly so:

---

130 W.J. Olson (1985) "The Light Force Initiative," *Military Review*, vol. 65 (no. 6), p. 4.

131 M. Ganley (1985) "Are Soldiers Headed for 'Hot' Spots Doomed to Train at Frigid Fort Drum?" *Armed Forces Journal International*, vol. 122 (no. 10), p. 78.

132 M.R. Gordon (1984) "The Charge of the Light Infantry: Army Plans Forces for Third World Conflicts," *National Journal*, vol. 16, May 19, p. 971.

133 R. Halloran (1985) "Light Infantry Divisions Give Army a New Force," *New York Times*, June 6, p. B16.

134 M. Ganley (1985) "Are Soldiers Headed for 'Hot' Spots Doomed to Train at Frigid Fort Drum?" *Armed Forces Journal International*, vol. 122 (no. 10), p. 80.

1) Offensive forces intended for "brush fire" wars in Southwest Asia, Africa, and Latin America, especially Central America, are being equipped and trained in winter conditions.

2) At a time when Federal deficits were a major concern and when cheaper alternative sites and surplus bases were available, the United States spent over $1,000,000,000 for the biggest Army construction project since World War II and gave it unprecedented advance budget authorization.

3) A division base was chosen a) for rapid deployment overseas even though the base lacks a suitable airfield and is noted for severe local weather; b) for regional economic development even though alternative regions were considerably poorer; and c) for the space to hold the entire division even though a full brigade was to be elsewhere and the base is now overcrowded.

Such anomalies in the public explanations and justifications for the basing of the 10th Mountain Division at Fort Drum inspire doubt and raise questions about the true purpose of those forces. Considering the very high priority the United States has on minimizing its combat casualities, it is just not believable that light infantry would be flown off to remote wars as "Kleenex" divisions. Considering the plethora of criticisms in US military journals of the Fort Drum basing, it is simply beyond belief that the Pentagon did not notice the difficulties.

CHAPTER 4

CAPABILITY TO ATTACK CANADA

CAUSE FOR CONCERN

The Fort Drum forces are most unusual. They are offensive, assault forces, specializing in rapid attack, surprise, stealth and night combat. They are training for winter warfare. They are training for urban, house-to-house fighting. They cannot face armoured forces. They cannot enter by force into a country with defended borders. They cannot have long or endangered resupply lines. They do not have ready or reliable access to an airfield for rapid overseas deployment. Where might a military force with these characteristics, based at Fort Drum, reasonably be expected to be used?

If the 10th Division seems ill-suited and ill-situated for its avowed mission of rapid deployment to political instabilities in the Third World, it would seem ideally suited and situated for rapid deployment against political "instabilities" in Canada that might threaten US interests. It is not difficult to imagine a number of developments that the United States might perceive as threatening. Some possibilities are: turmoil and violence caused by the independence of Quebec; restrictions on gas, oil, electricity or water exports to the United States at times of shortage; or perhaps even the election of a government in Ottawa seeking to restore Canadian sovereignty by abrogating the Free Trade Agreement, withdrawing from NORAD, or curbing the operations of major US corporations in Canada.

If Fort Drum forces were ever to be used against Canada, their military role would probably be to exert pressure by their very presence and preparation, or perhaps to actually intervene in an independent Quebec, or at extremes to remove a government in Ottawa that adopted policies contrary to US plans for North America. From a US perspective, if worse comes to worst, a quick intervention or even the show of force of the capability of that intervention, might well "snuff out" the crisis and preclude escalation to a larger intervention that would prove more costly in both political and military terms.

Fort Drum is the nearest US Army base to Ottawa and Montreal. Although the 10th Division might have difficulty transporting its entire divisional structure overseas, it would have no difficulty using its helicopters and light vehicles to send its rapid assault brigades into Canada. Although the 10th Division might be inadequate in the face of prepared defences and armoured forces, the Canadian border is undefended and without armoured backup.

The 10th Division itself, however, is backed by the 50th Armored Division, whose heavy equipment and deployment are under Fort Drum's command.[135] Despite all of the criticisms of light infantry as stand-alone forces, light infantry in combination with armoured forces are a uniquely powerful combination. Fort Drum staff have been at the forefront of developing tactics and command integration for complementary force operations. A division commander, Major-

---

[135] Anon. (1988) *10th Mountain Division (L.I.) and Fort Drum: An Unofficial Directory and Guide Published for Fort Drum Newcomers*, South Boston, VI: B. Hunt Enterprises.

General Peter Boylan,[136] and a brigade commanding officer, Colonel Wolf Kutter,[137] have both written about such operations. There are no military forces Canada could muster to counter a one-two combination punch by a light' division and an armoured division. The Fort Drum forces are also well within range of tactical air support from US air bases at Rome, Plattsburgh and Syracuse, N.Y. and at several New England sites.

In testimony to the Senate Armed Services Committee on February 5, 1985, Army Chief of Staff General John A. Wickham was asked by Senator Jeff Bingaman (Democrat, New Mexico), "Why is it not possible to use an existing base to accomplish what needs to be done at Fort Drum?" Wickham answered that Fort Drum "is an existing base" which has "a strategic location" that will assist in the division's deployment.[138] Considering the inadequacies of Fort Drum as a base for overseas deployment, the question is, "strategic" for what?

Certainly, Fort Drum is strategically located for managing Canada. Situated near the Thousand Islands, the base sits right on the natural geographic breaking point of central Canada. Geologically, the Thousand Islands are part of a southern extension of the Canadian Shield. The Frontenac Axis, as this extension is known, touches and crosses the border at this point. This is a region defined by the surface exposure of the ancient mass of crystalline rock that is the foundation of North America. In other parts of the continent, this rock is buried as much as 3000 meters (about 10,000 feet) deep.[139] The Canadian Shield and the Frontenac Axis are heavily glaciated and scraped clean of all but a thin soil. Settlement and population growth have naturally avoided such

---

[136] Major-General P.J. Boylan (1990) "Complementary Force Operations," *Military Review*, 70, June, pp. 27-37.

[137] Colonel W.D. Kutter (1990) "Deep Behind Enemy Lines," *Military Review*, 70, June, pp. 38-49.

[138] M. Ganley (1985) "Are Soldiers Headed for 'Hot' Spots Doomed to Train at Frigid Fort Drum?" *Armed Forces Journal International*, vol. 122 (no. 10), p. 80.

[139] E.P. Neufeld (1971) "Canada," *Encyclopedia Britannica* (vol. 4, pp. 726-761), London: William Benton.

terrain. Whether by intention or not, Fort Drum is a military wedge poised to strike into a natural fissure of Canadian geography and development.

Slightly to the east, well within the sights of Fort Drum, is the major ethnic fissure of Canada. The border between Ontario and Quebec marks the political breaking point of English Canada and French Canada. This is also the divide separating Canada's two major population centres, Toronto to the west, Montreal to the east. As historical accounts show, US military planners have long known the Thousand Islands region to be Canada's weakest point of defence. It is by hostile design — not by coincidence or inadvertency — that the United States first developed a military base at Fort Drum.

Without considering motivation or intention, looking only at the objective facts of location, capability and history, it is easy to conclude that the geopolitical, strategic purpose of Fort Drum's light infantry is rapid intervention into Canada. The military seizure of the region north of Fort Drum would simultaneously: 1) immobilize the Canadian national government; 2) disrupt Canadian military communications now centered at the Canadian Forces Base in Kingston; 3) sever east-west highway, railway, and seaway transportation in Canada; 4) split Canada at its major ethnic fissure; and 5) separate central Canada's two major population centres. Not bad for starters. Not bad for a day's work by a single division.

DISARMING ALLIANCE

Of course, many people on both sides of the border find this an unimaginable scenario. Canada and the United States, they think, have not been military antagonists for over a century and are now close allies in NATO and NORAD. In fact, Canadian air defences are under US military command.[140] The elimination of national

[140] P. Resnick (1970) "Canadian Defence Policy and the American Empire," in I. Lumsden (ed.), *Close the 49th Parallel Etc.: The Americanization of Canada* (pp. 93-115), Toronto: University of Toronto Press.

boundaries between the United States and Canada in matters of defence has been recommended in order to enhance the integration of Canada into the US military-industrial complex.[141] Indeed, Canada has less and less military independence from the United States every year. According to one Canadian analyst:

> ... what one saw in the press stories last year [1988] was the spectre of Canada slipping, sector by sector, into increasing integration with the United States. First free trade, then common market in defence products, then common defence policies, then other areas of national life, until little true independence was left.[142]

The two countries are the world's largest trading partners and are currently in the process of consolidating economic integration. A US attack on Canada appears to be unthinkable and unnecessary. Canada is not a Grenada or a Panama, but a major country. Would not a US attack on Canada be totally unacceptable to other major countries of the world?

At the present time, thinking only of recent decades of alliance and easy affluence, yes, it would seem to be an unbelievable scenario. Even laughable. However, looking at a longer stretch of history, or looking into an uncertain future, the humour fades.

In the nineteenth century, when the military defence of Canada from US attack was an active consideration, Eastern Ontario was considered critical, if not central, to Canadian national defence.[143] A large and costly system of military defences was built in this region for good reason. Although Fort Henry is now only an attraction for American tourists, its original purpose was quite different. Historically, Canada has had to defend itself from the United States.[144] Even into the 1920s and 1930s, Canada maintained

[141] A. Bryans (1988) "In our Worst Defence Interests," *Whig-Standard*, Nov. 17, p. 4.
[142] R. Hill (1989) "Unified Canada-US Defence Production: A Hazardous Road," *Canadian Institute for International Peace and Security*, vol. 4 (no. 2), p. 5.
[143] W.H. Russell (1865) *Canada: Its Defence, Condition and Resources*, London: Bradbury and Evans.
[144] K. Bourne (1967) *Britain and the Balance of Power in North America, 1815-1908*, Berkeley, CA: University of California Press.
  (footnote continued next page)

defensive plans against US threats of invasion and US violations of Canadian neutrality.[145] In international relations, enemies and allies can change rather fast. For example, in 1945 Germany and Japan were our most hated enemies and the Soviet Union was an ally. However, within a relatively short time those roles had reversed. International events can change faster than habits of thought or memories of alliance.

It should also be remembered that no modern invasions are considered by the aggressors to be acts of "aggression." They always call their military actions "defensive" or "humanitarian." Invasions are proclaimed to be for the benefit of, or even by the invitation of, the people being invaded. The stories are familiar: the Soviet Union's invasions of Hungary, Czechoslovakia and Afghanistan; the United States' invasions of Vietnam, Grenada and Panama; Vietnam's invasion of Cambodia; China's invasion of Tibet; India's invasions of Goa and Pakistan; Syria's and Israel's invasions of Lebanon; Indonesia's invasion of East Timor. Saddam Hussein failed to appreciate the importance of benevolent justifications for invasions of neighbouring states.

The use of the 10th Mountain Division in Canada, if the time comes, would certainly be construed as benevolent by the United States, perhaps by other nations and even by many Canadians. Certainly, the use of US troops in Canada would have to be engineered to appear to Americans to benefit Canadians, since the deep goodwill and respect for Canada in the United States would not allow an unmitigated act of aggression. The necessary manipulations of public opinion would be arranged. The 10th Division would surely come into Canada by "invitation" as an act of "friendship" to "stabilize" a political "crisis" and to support a "close ally" in fulfilment of "treaty obligations." There is little

R.C. Stuart (1988) *United States Expansionism and British North America, 1775-1871*, Chapel Hill, NC: University of North Carolina Press.
[145] J. Eayrs (1964) *In Defence of Canada* (vol. 1), Toronto: University of Toronto Press.

question that the United States would be in a position to extract consent to these terms from a dependent Canadian government.

Newspaper reports on this concern about Fort Drum have frequently used the word "invasion." For example, the *Watertown Daily Times* headlined a column, "Invasion of Canada," and even fabricated a quotation saying, "It would take them a week to take all of Canada."[146] People probably envision massed armies and rows of tanks and aircraft sweeping across the borders, east to west, and say the idea is simply ridiculous. Although the United States made preparations for such an invasion in earlier decades, that is not a scenario which has ever been suggested of the Fort Drum forces. In fact, given the size of Canada, given Canada's winter conditions and given the inability of the United States to defend seized resource lines, a fullblown invasion and military occupation of Canada would be a costly failure, even if militarily unopposed. Much of the civilian population would be resistant, and an occupied Canada could well become a Northern Ireland on a continental scale.

Light infantry were designed for rapid interventions so as to preclude the need for large scale invasions. In the "New World Order," interventions must be quick, contained, and politically palatable. Surgical strike is the idea. Surprise attack and stealth. Take control of a few key points. "Pre-response," "insertion of defensive capability," "limited assistance" are the tacticians' preferred expressions, not "invasion."

The rationale for developing light infantry was to prepare military interventions that would be precise, preemptive and politically acceptable.[147] To use the military terminology and acronyms, light

---

[146] J. Golden (1990) "Invasion of Canada? He's Serious," *Watertown Daily Times*, April 8, pp. C1-C2.

[147] M.T. Klare and P. Kornbluh (1988) "The New Interventionism: Low-Intensity Warfare in the 1980's and Beyond," in M. Klare and P. Kornbluh (eds.), *Low-Intensity Warfare* (pp. 3-20), New York: Pantheon Books.

M.R. Gordon (1984) "The Charge of the Light Infantry: Army Plans Forces for Third World Conflicts," *National Journal*, vol. 16, May 19, pp. 968-972.

W.J. Olson (1985) "The Light Force Initiative," *Military Review*, vol. 65 (no. 6), pp. 2-17.

infantry are specifically designed for "Low-Intensity Conflicts" (LIC) and for "Foreign Internal Defense" (FID).[148] Often these require only a show of force. Military planning documents for light infantry state:

If force cannot be avoided, then combat forces are to be used "at decisive points for specific payoffs" rather than a possible long-term sustained effort.[149]

A light infantry division at Fort Drum, backed by a reserve armoured division, is well-situated for limited intervention in Canada. Furthermore such a force would not require staging preparations that might give away imminent deployment. There would already be down in the parkas and antifreeze in the vehicles. Everything would be ready.

PORK-BARRELLING

To some who examine US military spending, it is generally misguided to try to deduce any military intentions at all from the facts of US military preparations. These critics would argue that the processes and purposes of military appropriations have little to do with actual strategic planning and that US defence spending is an uncontrolled interaction of bureaucratic, business, and political interests.[150] The process is so complex with so much argument, testimony, and conflicting information from so many competing interests that almost any theory of US intentions might find supporting evidence in almost any military appropriation. Thus, it might be argued that the decision to base the 10th Division at Fort

---

[148] M.M. Zais (1986) "LIC: Matching Mission and Forces," *Military Review*, vol. 66 (no. 8), pp. 79-88.

[149] Major P.N. Kafkalas (1986) "The Light Divisions and the Low-Intensity Conflict: Are They Losing Sight of Each Other?" *Military Review*, vol. 66 (no. 1), p. 21. This quote is citing *US Army Interim Operational Concept for Low Intensity Conflict*, Low-Intensity Conflict Committee, US Army Command and General Staff College (USACGSC), Fort Leavenworth, Kansas, undated, p. 34.

[150] F. Hiatt and R. Atkinson (1985) "To Pentagon, Oversight has become Overkill," *Washington Post*, July 4, p. A1, A12.

M.R. Gordon (1984) "The Charge of the Light Infantry: Army Plans Forces for Third World Conflicts," *National Journal*, vol. 16, May 19, pp. 968-972.

Drum can be fully explained, and perhaps best explained, by Congressional pork-barrelling, bureaucratic self-interest and business lobbying.

"Pork-barrelling" is a US slang expression meaning "a government appropriation, bill, or policy which supplies funds for local improvements designed to ingratiate legislators with their constituents."[151] It may be that a Republican administration wanted to secure a district of northern New York as a Republican stronghold. The economic benefits of a new divisional military base would reward past Republican electoral victories and ensure that they would continue into the future.

However, a billion dollar base would seem unnecessary for that. The *Congressional Directory* shows that the district that includes the Fort Drum region has voted Republican for decades, even during Barry Goldwater's crushing defeat in the 1964 Presidential election. Congressman Martin won by more than two-to-one in 1980 and 1982, elections which occurred before the decision to base the 10th Division at Fort Drum. In addition, much of the political lobbying for that decision was done by Democrats, support which Congressman Martin publicly acknowledged in his news release announcing the Army's decision to base the 10th Division at Fort Drum:

I am indebted to the entire New York State Congressional Delegation for its support, particularly Senator Alfonse M. D'Amato and Rep. Samuel S. Stratton. New York State has made substantial commitments to our cause, and I am grateful to Gov. Mario M. Cuomo ... [152]

It may be that New York politicians were able to muster enough political muscle to force the decision upon the Pentagon,[153] or that the Pentagon chose Fort Drum willingly in order to create a New

---

[151] *Random House Dictionary of the English Language* (unabridged edition, edited by Jesse Stein), New York: Random House, 1981, p. 1119.
[152] Received from Congressman Martin's office, Oct. 4, 1988.
[153] A. Emory (1984) "Martin's Persistence, Army Outlook Landed 10th," *Watertown Daily Times*, Dec. 13, p. 10.

FLOYD RUDMIN

York State constituency in Congress,[154] or that the creation of light infantry allows the Army to have more divisions for the same total manpower[155] However, all US military appropriations will show evidence of Congressional pork-barrelling and Pentagon bureaucratic self-interest. These explain nothing. If something appears everywhere, it has little explanatory power. A death is not explained by noting that the corpse is not breathing. A Pentagon decision is not explained by noting that someone benefitted.

Pork-barrelling is an old and well-established tradition in Washington, with professionals in and out of government who specialize in its methods. Military planning must proceed despite, *or by means of*, appeal to pork-barrelling and special interests. The fact that many and various political and bureaucratic motivations might have been satisfied by the development of light infantry and the basing of the 10th Division at Fort Drum does not mean that there is no military or strategic rationale for those forces. That various regions, groups, or individuals might have profited from the decision to base offensive forces at Fort Drum does not mean that those forces are benign and beyond criticism or concern.

A MATTER OF TRUST

It is difficult for Canadians to make an impartial, dispassionate consideration of national defence vis-à-vis the United States. Concerns that the offensive troops at Fort Drum are directed towards Canada may seem unbalanced on the paranoid side. Dismissal of those concerns as merely paranoid is unbalanced on the naive side. The difference is in the readiness to trust or distrust the forces that govern the United States.

---

[154] M. Weisskopf (1985) "Community Happily Anticipates Army Invasion," *Washington Post*, May 27, p. A3.
[155] M.R. Gordon (1984) "The Charge of the Light Infantry: Army Plans Forces for Third World Conflicts," *National Journal*, vol. 16, May 19, pp. 968-972.

When concerns about the developments at Fort Drum were first presented to the office of the Honourable Flora MacDonald, Member of Parliament for Kingston and the Islands, the staff member who accepted the letter surmised that the Fort Drum forces must be for NATO deployment. She added that her husband is in the Canadian Forces, is friends with US military personnel, and "just knows" that the United States would not make military preparations against Canada.[156] The letter was eventually forwarded to the Honourable Perrin Beatty, then Minister of Defence, who responded that he presumes that the Fort Drum troops are suitable for winter warfare in Europe. He found confidence in the fact that Canada and the United States are "trusted partners in such collective security arrangements as the North Atlantic Treaty Organization and the North American Aerospace Defence."[157]

Statements such as these represent the trusting side. On the distrusting side are those Canadian analysts who look at the "Realpolitik" of Canada-US relations. For example, in 1970, political scientist Philip Resnick wrote on "Canadian Defence Policy and the American Empire." He concluded: "The real threat to Canada since 1945 has come from the south, not the north."[158] Perhaps the strongest contemporary voices of concern come from those Canadians who steadfastly oppose the Canada-US Free Trade Agreement.[159] For example, David Orchard, a western farmer and leader of Citizens Concerned About Free Trade, wrote a pamphlet entitled *Free Trade: The Full Story*. He begins with a history of US expansionism against Canada by force and by treaty. He suggests that the United States might still use military force against its North American neighbours should treaty arrangements

---

[156] Personal communication, Oct. 22, 1987.

[157] P. Beatty (1988) Personal letter, January 7.

[158] P. Resnick (1970) "Canadian Defence Policy and the American Empire," in I. Lumsden (ed.), *Close the 49th Parallel Etc.: The Americanization of Canada* (pp. 93-115)., Toronto: University of Toronto Press, p. 113.

[159] M. Barlow (1991) *Parcel of Rogues: How Free Trade is Failing Canada* (revised), Toronto: Key Porter.

not satisfy its interests. In his discussion of Mexico's free trade zone along the border, Orchard wrote:

During their negotiations with the US, Mexico asked for the inclusion in the agreement of an American promise not to use military intervention to enforce any trade disputes. The United States refused to agree.[160]

---

[160] D. Orchard (1988) *Free Trade: The Full Story*, Saskatoon, SK: Patriots Press, p. 37.

CHAPTER 5

CONSPIRACY, CONTINGENCY OR MISTAKE

From a Canadian perspective, there are a number of possible explanations for the new presence of an offensive assault force on the border. These explanations range from the very distrusting to the more matter-of-fact.

CONSPIRACY

At the most suspicious end of the spectrum is the explanation that a rightwing conspiracy within the Reagan-Bush administration manipulated military policies and decisions as part of a larger plan to secure the longterm economic and political integration of North America under US control. Basing light infantry at Fort Drum would be a piece of the military backup for that plan. Of course, consideration of conspiracy presumes that those involved will leave little clear evidence of their intentions or actions and that they will even arrange plausible counterevidence in order to maintain deniability. Nevertheless, for those with an open mind, the evidence for conspiracy is credible, if only circumstantial.

First there is the fact that rightwing conspiracies were an integral part of the Reagan-Bush administration. The Iran-Contra Affair is very well known by name, although the full extent and depth of the crime and corruption may never be revealed. For example, it may be that not only President George Bush but also his Democratic successor were both involved in the Iran-Contra machinations. There are reports that Bill Clinton as Governor of Arkansas may have abetted the smuggling of guns south and drugs north via state-financed front-companies using the airfield at Mena, Arkansas.[161] Another Reagan-Bush conspiracy now coming to light is known as "The October Surprise." This concerns the 1980 conspiracy and coverup by CIA director Casey, then head of the Reagan-Bush election campaign, to covertly negotiate with Iranian clerics to block the release of American hostages in order to thwart the re-election bid of President Jimmy Carter.[162]

Probably least well-known of the Reagan-Bush conspiracies so far exposed is "REX 84." According to a 1988 Federal Court affidavit prepared by Daniel P. Sheehan for the Christic Institute, a public interest law firm and policy centre in Washington, D.C.,[163] "REX 84" was the code word for a martial law plan, authorized on April 6, 1984, by National Security Decision Directive #52. By this plan, arms and ammunition would be transferred by the Federal Emergency Management Agency (FEMA) from State National Guard units to ultra-rightwing, civilian State Defense Forces. "REX 84" also entailed preparations for the arrest of some 400,000 Central American refugees and for their confinement in military

---

[161] A. Cockburn (1992) "Beat the Devil," *The Nation*, Feb. 24, pp. 222-223.

A. Cockburn (1992) "Beat the Devil," *The Nation*, April 6, pp. 438-439.

[162] G. Sick (1991) *October Surprise: America's Hostages in Iran and the Election of Ronald Reagan*, New York: Times Books/Random House.

G. Sick, (1992) *A Question of Treason: America's Hostages and the Election of Ronald Reagan*, New York: Times Books/Random House.

[163] Information from the Christic Institute, in Washington, D.C. was sent Jan. 30, 1988.

concentration camps. Fort Drum was one of the ten centres designated to hold large numbers of civilian detainees.

A second cause for suspicion of conspiracy is the fact that the conservative political forces behind Ronald Reagan's Presidency did have plans to forge a North American union. Pursuit of those plans was not always explicit and forthright. T.H. White, the chronicler of US presidential elections, noted that when Reagan announced his candidacy on November 8, 1979, he held out "as the centerpiece of his future foreign policy a North American community of Canada, Mexico, and the United States, *a proposal never again to be mentioned in his campaign*" (emphasis added).[164] By the end of his two terms, Reagan had succeeded in establishing a comprehensive "free trade" agreement with Canada and a "free trade" zone in Mexico. He called the Canada-US Free Trade Agreement "a new economic constitution for North America" and likened it to the US Constitution when it bound together the thirteen colonies into an economic and political union.[165]

A third cause for concern about conspiracy is the fact that the 10th Division was created outside the usual Pentagon procedures and bureaucratic channels. Light infantry divisions were first announced in the 1985 defense budget submitted to Congress in January 1984. Congress was surprised and sceptical. Congressman Addabbo, a representative from New York State later to be credited with lobbying for Fort Drum,[166] was initially uninformed and unsupportive:

The single most significant program change may well be the Army proposal to create a new active light infantry division. It is proposed that the necessary 10,000 personnel for this division will come from within the existing force

---

[164] T.H. White (1982) *America in Search of Itself: The Making of the President 1956-1980*, New York: Harper and Row, p. 14.

[165] R. Reagan (1987) "Speech to New Jersey Chamber of Commerce: Oct. 13, 1987." *Weekly Compilation of Presidential Documents* vol. 23, no. 41, pp. 1162-1166, quoting from p. 1165.

[166] M. Weisskopf (1985) "Community Happily Anticipates Army Invasion," *Washington Post*, May 27, p. A3.

structure despite past testimony from the Army that existing units are short of personnel.[167]

There was apparently good reason for this surprise, as reported in 1985 by Michael Gordon:

The Army did not supply much advance warning of its plans. The light divisions were not mentioned in a program objective memorandum that was drafted last May [1984] in preparation for the 1985 budget, nor was the plan mentioned in a later proposed budget that was circulated in the Pentagon last September.

Army officials say that the plans were discussed during August and October conferences of top Army commanders. The first formal presentation of the plans came in November ...

The Army plan also caught others in the Administration by surprise, including officials at the national security division of the Office of Management and Budget (OMB) and at the National Security Council. "It happened late in the budget season and was never really fully examined here," said a White House official. OMB took the position that the Army's plans could not be reflected in the fiscal 1985 budget without President Reagan's approval because they involved structural changes in the Army forces that had foreign policy implications.[168]

Despite the Army's claim, some top military commanders were not consulted about the light divisions. For example, General Howard Stone, then head of the Army's European Command, testified to Senator Tower in 1985 that his command was not consulted and that he doubts the utility of light infantry in the European theatre.[169]

The development of light infantry divisions is seen to have been General John Wickham's initiative upon taking over as Army Chief of Staff. The sudden budget allocation for light infantry is seen to have been "politically adroit" and "an end run around most of the Pentagon."[170] Such accounts are speculation to explain aberration.

[167] J.P. Addabbo (1984) "Analysis of Fiscal Year 1985 Defense Budget," *Congressional Record*, vol. 130 (no. 9), Feb. 2, pp. H439-H443, quoting from p. H441.
[168] M.R. Gordon (1984) "The Charge of the Light Infantry: Army Plans Forces for Third World Conflicts," *National Journal*, vol. 16, May 19, p. 970.
[169] M.R. Gordon (1985) "Army's Third World Strike Force Finds a Home — in Alaska of All Cold Places," *National Journal*, vol. 7, April 14, p. 728.
[170] M.R. Gordon (1984) "The Charge of the Light Infantry: Army Plans Forces for Third World Conflicts," *National Journal*, vol. 16, May 19, p. 969.

Even if true, it is not clear who was "calling the play" in this successful attempt to by-pass normal planning procedures.

A final point suggesting conspiracy is that Fort Drum seems to have been a predetermined site for a new assault force. As a first-year Congressman, Mr. Martin was called to a private meeting with the President and Secretary of Defense late in 1981 and was promised more base construction than his higher ranking predecessor could acquire in years of effort, all for not complaining about Haitian detainees.[171] It is important to bear in mind that power in Congress is a function of tenure and that such meetings and promises are not common for first-year Congressmen.

The Pentagon did not make its request for a new light infantry division until January, 1984. Approximately six months later, the *Army Times* predicted, "with almost total accuracy," the decision to base light infantry at Fort Drum.[172] Apparently that rumour was well established in Washington. For example, one military journal article, written before the final decision to base light infantry at Fort Drum, said:

A decision will be made, probably in the last quarter of this year, on where the second light division will be headquartered. Among the candidates are Fort Drum (New York), Fort Lewis (Arkansas), Fort Benning (Georgia), Fort Ord [California], and Fort Campbell (Kentucky), or a combination of two of these sites. Fort Drum is expected to receive at least a portion.[173]

These indications of prior design support suspicion that the decision to base light infantry at Fort Drum *caused*, rather than *was caused by*, the political lobby that is credited with that decision. In military appropriations, if a prize is dangled out front, the motivations of those rushing to get it should not be confused with the motivations of those arranging events behind the curtains.

---

[171] A. Emory (1984) "Martin's Persistence, Army Outlook Landed 10th," *Watertown Daily Times*, Dec. 13, p. 10.
[172] Ibid.
[173] T. Velocci (1984) "The New Light Division: Will It Work?" *National Defense*, vol. 69 (no. 402), Nov., p. 57.

Of course, a conspiracy theory gains most credence from the unbelievability of official explanations for the development of light infantry and the basing of one division at Fort Drum. Considering the actual capabilities of the new light infantry divisions and the actual location of Fort Drum, it does not require paranoia to suspect that a realistic mission is the future military management of Canada. The United States has created rapid attack forces with special preparation in seizing undefended cities in times of crisis and has placed one division of those forces within easy striking range of Ottawa and Montreal.

CONTINGENCY PLANNING

More mundane than conspiracy is the explanation that light infantry were based at Fort Drum as part of routine and professional military contingency planning. From the perspective of US strategic planners, it might well seem necessary that they have sufficient forces, of the appropriate type, based at suitable sites, to maintain civil order both within the United States and in the immediately neighbouring nations in which it has important, longstanding economic interests. If the United States were to prepare and station assault troops near the border for future military contingencies against Canada, they would be most effective if they were in place and well-accepted years — even decades — before they might be used. It is possible that the creation of new light infantry divisions and the basing of the 10th Mountain Division at Fort Drum are neither externally manipulated, nor politically skewed, nor muddled decisions, but rather very reasonable decisions suited to longterm US interests in North America.

From one perspective, this may be conceived as aggressive, interventionist, Monroe Doctrine intimidation. The former executive officers who comprise the Center for Defense Information have concluded that light infantry divisions are intended for internal security operations and for participation in coups d'etat:

Indeed the lack of firepower has led many to speculate that the LID could not be effective against the regular military forces of most Third World governments. Thus, its primary role would necessarily be to support Third World governments against rebels. Yet LIDs may not really be suited for guerrilla warfare either. It might be that LIDs will be effective only for a small range of situations — suppressing coup d'etats or limited internal security operations — and little else.[174]

A US Army War College analyst has similarly emphasized the role of light infantry in coups:

One of its underlying purposes was a show of force that might forestall an insurgency or a coup. In this sense, the LID is an instrument for promoting stability which reinforces the policy aspect of the instrument.[175]

Coups d'etat usually occur in national capitals. Whether a military force is perceived as preventing a coup d'etat or performing one depends on what the rival claims of legitimacy are, who issues the invitation for outside intervention, and which side wins.

From a different planning perspective, the preparation of rapid deployment light infantry assault forces on the Canadian border may be more "benevolent." If Quebec does decide to secede from Canada, there are various scenarios that would predict significant violence, civil disorder, even civil war. In November 1991, the Canadian Institute of Strategic Studies hosted a conference on the military implications of Quebec separation.[176] The most obvious scenarios for civil disorder or civil war are: 1) counterseparations from Quebec by native peoples or by English communities; 2) explosive nationalist or ethnic violence in Quebec; and 3) a failure to negotiate geographic and economic conditions of separation. The argument has also been made that unilateral secession by Quebec

[174] Rear-Admiral (retired) E.J. Carroll (1987) "Militarization, the Superpowers, and the Third World," presented at conference on *Militarization in the Third World*, Queen's University, Kingston, Ontario, January, 1987, p. 14.
[175] W.J. Olson (1985) "The Light Force Initiative," *Military Review*, vol. 65 (no. 6), p. 7.
[176] G. York (1991) "Experts Weigh Civil War Scenarios," *Globe and Mail*, Nov. 6, p. A6.
G. York (1991) "Quebec Violence after Vote Envisaged," *Globe and Mail*, Nov. 7, p. A4.
G. York (1991) "Canada could Require US Might, Analyst Says," *Globe and Mail*, Nov. 8, p. A3.
T. Walkom (1991) "Can We Really Rule Out Civil War?" *Toronto Star*, Nov. 11, p. A15.

is illegal and should be resisted by federal military forces.[177] It should be noted that Canada's former Minister of Defence, Marcel Masse, representing Quebec, moved a major military supply depot to Montreal.[178] It is not beyond possibility that this would secure for Quebec adequate military supplies in the event of civil war. More than 25% of Canadian military personnel are Quebeckers, and the Parti Québécois has demanded that at least that portion must be turned over to a sovereign Quebec.[179] Separatists predict that independence will be achieved by June 1995.[180]

If federal or provincial governments did need to use military force for secession scenarios, the Canadian Armed Forces would be unreliable and perhaps ineffective due to divided loyalties and splintering command structure. Peter Haydon, policy analyst and former naval commander, has said, "The federal government cannot depend on the loyalty of French-Canadian troops if violence erupts after a Quebec referendum [on sovereignty]...."[181] A reliable military force for the maintenance of civil order following secession would have to be non-Canadian. It is certain that Canadian and US military authorities have foreseen this eventuality. By location and capabilities, Fort Drum forces are ideal for such scenarios. In this line of speculation, it is plausible that a light infantry assault force is being readied at Fort Drum, not only by the sufferance of the Canadian military command, but by their active consent, or even at their request. If this line of speculation is correct, then Canadian sovereignty is a charade.

US military analysts have long believed that Canadian Armed Forces have a "Commitment-Capability Gap." Even in the best of

---

[177] D. Sanger (1991) "Use Army to Stop Quebec Separation, Lawyer Says," Whig-Standard, Nov. 27, p. 7.
[178] T. Harper (1992) "Military Depot Move Criticized by Redway," Toronto Star, March 31, p. A10.
[179] Anon. (1992) "Canada 'Would be Expected to Surrender Part of Military'," Calgary Herald, Dec. 17, p. A7.
[180] R. McKenzie (1992) "Quebec Will be Sovereign by June '95 PQ Predicts," Toronto Star, Dec. 22, p. A13.
[181] G. York (1991) "Quebec Violence after Vote Envisaged," Globe and Mail, Nov. 7, p. A4.

times Canada cannot meet its defence treaty obligations.[182] US analyst Joseph Jockel has said that it is quite evident that Canada is going to decentralize, either from successful constitutional negotiations with Quebec or as a consequence of Quebec independence. In either case, "Canada will be unable to maintain defences as it decentralizes."[183] The United States, Jockel argued, is prepared to provide military security for Canada and "would be prepared to insist on access to Canadian airspace, waters, and territories."[184] Professor J.L. Granatstein has made a quite similar argument with specific references to Fort Drum and Plattsburgh Air Force Base.[185] Analyses from the Brookings Institution predict that Canada is going to disintegrate and it is a reasonable inference that there will be violence for which the US will wish to have a military response ready.[186]

Canadian Brigadier-General (retired) Donald Macnamara, who was once in charge of strategic planning for the Canadian Armed Forces, has focused even more specifically on US forces at Fort Drum "helping" Canada defend the St. Lawrence Seaway. He has said several times that Fort Drum forces are "exactly right" for defending the St. Lawrence Seaway and might be "called into Canada" for that purpose:

I see perfectly logical, and even from a Canadian point of view, perfectly acceptable reasons for the United States to have forces stationed near Canada, either to assist Canada when Canada perceives that [it] may not be able to do these things for itself, or to defend its own interests, particularly territorial, in terms of Seaway protection.[187]

---

[182] J.T. Jockel (1991) *Security to the North: Canada-US Defense Relation in the 1990's*, East Lansing, Michigan: Michigan State University Press.

[183] G. York (1991) "Canada could Require US Might, Analyst Says," *Globe and Mail*, Nov. 8, p. A3.

[184] Ibid.

[185] J.L. Granatstein (1991) "Canada, Quebec and the World," chapter in J.L. Granatstein and K. McNaught (eds.), *"English Canada" Speaks Out*, Toronto: Doubleday.

[186] R.K. Weaver (Ed.) (1992) *The Collapse of Canada?*, Washington, DC: Brookings Institution.

[187] D. Hogan (1990) "Too Close for Comfort? Military Experts Divided on Theory Fort Drum May be a Threat to Canada," *Whig-Standard*, March 24, p. 4.

FLOYD RUDMIN

To the *Ottawa Citizen*, Macnamara said, "Even if they wanted to have troops to protect the St. Lawrence area there's nothing anti-Canadian about that."[188] If this attitude is pervasive in the Canadian military, then national sovereignty already has been surrendered.

Taking General Macnamara's scenario seriously, the only plausible threat to the St. Lawrence Seaway that could be used to justify intervention by US assault forces would be closure of the locks by Canadian or Quebec civil authorities, possibly in dispute with one another. Canadian historian Desmond Morton has predicted exactly this scenario. Talking about a sovereign Quebec contending in post-independence quarrels with Canada, he asked, "Will they resist the temptation to jerk at the St. Lawrence Seaway?"[189]

In this kind of discussion, it should be noted, Seaway defence is more an excuse than a valid reason for the deployment of military forces. The Seaway is closed by ice for much of the year, is too small for today's large ships and has declining traffic. It is hardly worth the expenditures of billions of dollars to have assault forces ready and waiting to open the locks. The money might better have been spent on canal improvement and maintenance.

To claim that Fort Drum forces are for Seaway defence also presumes that US military planners had enough foreknowledge in 1983 and 1984 to predict that Quebec separatism would soon be threatening the Seaway. In 1983, Quebec separatist sentiment was at a low of 23%, down from 40% at the time of the 1980 referendum.[190] Why begin spending billions to defend against a diminishing threat? However, if Fort Drum is part of a Reagan-era plan to consolidate North America and if individuals or agencies in the US security services have been actively arranging Quebec

---

[188] D. Pugliese (1990) "The Americans are Coming! The Americans are Coming!" *Ottawa Citizen*, Dec. 30, p. A1.
[189] G. York (1991) "Experts Weigh Civil War Scenarios," *Globe and Mail*, Nov. 6, p. A6.
[190] Anon. (1983) "Support Slumps for PQ's Option," *Montreal Gazette*, April 30, p. A1, A2.

separatism and Canadian decentralization, then maybe this is an instance of the right hand knowing what the left hand is doing.

In opposition to these discussions that Quebec separation might create situations resulting in US military intervention from Fort Drum, Joel Sokolsky, an associate professor of politics at Canada's Royal Military College in Kingston, has said:

It's one of the most ridiculous things that has ever been written on Canadian-US defense relations ... If Quebec separates, it would be done in such a way that vital American interests would not even remotely be jeopardized.[191]

However, US conservative political insiders such as Patrick Buchanan have been saying that the separation of Quebec *is* exactly what is most vital to American interests. Only then can the rest of Canada be comfortably absorbed.[192]

From still another perspective, it is realistic to presume that US military planners had no exact foreknowledge but could generally foresee in the mid-1980s that they might be called upon in the 1990s to secure civil order and to protect US interests in North America. William Olson of the US Army War College explained:

Despite some invidious questions that have been raised, the military is not looking for situations where it can send forces. The light force initiative is not an attempt to seek out new frontiers for war.

The military is aware, however, that US interests are potentially threatened and that it will be required to respond to protect those interests should the nation direct it to. It is also aware that it will be held responsible for any shortcomings, even if they were beyond its control or part of a political process that failed to provide adequate, consistent guidance or appropriate support.[193]

In basing the 10th Division at Fort Drum, perhaps the Pentagon may only have been trying to "do its job" of anticipating affronts to US interests and preparing violent responses. However, there

---

[191] J.D. Salant (1991) "The War that Never Was," *Post-Standard* (Syracuse), March 25, p. A4.

[192] P. Buchanan (1988) "Is Annexation of Canada in the Cards for the US?" *The Bangor Daily News*, Jan. 19, p. 10.

P. Buchanan (1990) "Canadian Disunity and the Rise of the American Empire" (excerpt), *Globe and Mail*, April 17, p. A7.

[193] W.J. Olson (1985) "The Light Force Initiative," *Military Review*, vol. 65 (no. 6), p. 16.

should be no excuses that US military planning is a passive victim of inadequate, inconsistent political guidance and inappropriate support. As Richard Preston has so well documented, the subversion of constitutional civilian political authority by military secrecy and misinformation has been endemic in the United States for more than a century, particularly when it comes to preparing for war against Canada.[194]

The US military depends upon the strength of the US economy. During the 1980s, the United States experienced deteriorating economic infrastructures, declining productivity, declining competitiveness, and record trade and public spending deficits. These changed the United States in a few years from the world's greatest creditor nation to its biggest debtor nation. Furthermore, world geopolitics are definitely in transition. As communism and Russia have declined as the principle challenge for the United States, a united Europe and a powerful East Asia have arisen. Furthermore, global ecological damage is causing historically unprecedented problems with totally unknown consequences to world economies and present geopolitical relationships. At a time when the US economy is unstable, when its own resources are depleted and foreign resources are becoming scarce and uncertain, when world geopolitical relationships are in transition, when the future is no longer predictable, in such a period of flux, assured access by the United States to Canadian resources would be a comfort worth planning for.

This has been articulated within US strategic planning circles. For example, *Parameters: Journal of the US Army War College* carried an article explaining that US political leaders became convinced in the early 1980s of the need to secure vital US interests in North America:

---

[194] R.A. Preston (1977) *The Defence of the Undefended Border: Planning for War in North America 1867-1939.* Montreal: McGill-Queen's University Press.

73

First of all, the United States has such a high intensity of interest in Canada and the Caribbean Basin that it should not compromise with military threats to any part of this area ... The United States also has a vital interest in preserving its trade and investments with the North American countries and its access to the energy resources and raw materials of Canada, Jamaica, Mexico, and Venezuela.[195]

It is claimed that Canada has a unique affinity for the United States and a uniquely trusting special relationship:

In sum, Canada and the United States form one of the strongest bonds of friendship on basic defense and foreign policy matters existing between neighboring countries anywhere in the world ... The consensus that exists in the northern part of North America does not, however, extend to the southern region — Mexico, Central America, the islands of the Caribbean, and the northern tier of South America. These countries have a strong national interest in resisting US encroachment on their sovereignty ... Unlike Canadians, who know that the US government will not send troops to Canada unless there is an attack from outside North America, the people and governments south of the US border have no such confidence.[196]

The article states that "Few Americans doubt that the United States has vital interests in Canada" and cites Prime Minister Trudeau's acquiescence to US cruise missile testing in 1983 "despite strong public protests" by Canadians.[197]

"OOPS" IS NO ANSWER

Finally, let us suppose that the inferences and implications thus far expressed about Fort Drum are all simply wrong; that the official explanations given by the United States for the basing of the 10th Mountain Division at Fort Drum are indeed the true and correct explanations; or, that the Fort Drum forces are there by accident, purely as a result of political pork-barrelling and bureaucratic bungling, just a mistake. Let us suppose that the US military truly

---

[195] D.E. Nuechterlein (1985) "North America: Our Neglected Heartland," *Parameters: Journal of the US Army War College*, vol. 15 (no. 3), pp. 58-65, quoting from pp. 62-63.
[196] Ibid., p. 60.
[197] Ibid, pp.59-60.

never had, and does not now have, any intentions of using the expanded Fort Drum forces for threats or actions against Canada and that compelling arguments can be raised against any and all reasons for the United States to consider military contingencies against Canada.

The fact still remains that rapid attack troops are now garrisoned on an undefended border, 130 kilometers (80 miles) from Canada's national capital. Considering the nature of the new light infantry divisions, that fact alone, without any consideration of prior intentions, is worrisome. Because light infantry are intended to preempt a political crisis and because their capabilities are drastically diminished if they face prepared defenses, light infantry are not likely to be used with caution. This has been emphasized by Rear-Admiral (retired) Eugene Carroll: "LIDs will be most useful if deployed *before* hostilities begin."[198]

There is a fine line between stopping a crisis by preemptive intervention and starting the crisis by that very intervention. Several analysts have discussed this. Said Carroll:

The major problem with the LID in the future may be the simple fact that it exists. Once the US has rapid reaction forces in place, the temptation will be great to use them, without taking sufficient time to consider objectives, costs and risks, and without recognizing the limitations and constraints of LIDs. The Army's approach to LIDs seems to be: get there fast and ask questions later.[199]

Michael Klare, writing in the *Nation*, said:

There is another danger not being voiced by the dissenters: the availability of rapidly deployable units of this sort will encourage US officials to intervene in future conflicts ... Although the existence of an option does not necessarily mean that Washington would automatically exercise it in a crisis, the Vietnam War and the invasion of Grenada suggest that a capacity for intervention tends to be accompanied by a propensity for such action. "If it is easy for us to go

---

[198] Rear-Admiral (retired) E.J. Carroll (1987) "Militarization, the Superpowers, and the Third World," presented at conference on *Militarization in the Third World*, Queen's University, Kingston, Ontario, January, 1987, p. 14.
[199] Ibid.

somewhere and do anything," Senator Richard B. Russell once observed, "we will always be going somewhere and doing something." [200]

It has further been noted that any use of light infantry in hasty, rapid deployment scenarios will inevitably lead to escalation:

The Army's light infantry divisions appear to be nothing more than a mobile tripwire for another Vietnam, or something a whole lot worse. [201]

Said another military analyst:

The purpose of the LID is to respond quickly, but it is not a stand alone force beyond certain contingencies. Should circumstances require, the LID will be, will have to be, reinforced. Putting aside the question of available [air] lift, this situation implies an escalation process. If the LID runs into trouble and must be reinforced, the decision to escalate will become virtually automatic. [202]

If the creation of light infantry and the basing of a division at Fort Drum are indeed accidents of Congressional pork-barrelling and military bureaucracy, then the 10th Division at Fort Drum is a military force looking for a rationale and a mission. There is a risk that it will find these by looking north. The US basing of the 10th Division at Fort Drum shows insensitivity toward Canada at best, hostility at worst.

Rapid-deployment light infantry were conceived and created under the Reagan-Bush administration, which showed a consistent, ideological preference for the development, deployment and use of military force in international relations. Les Aspin, in a 1984 retrospective analysis of the Reagan administration's rationale for invading Grenada, concluded:

In sum, the invasion of Grenada reveals two things and two things only. It reveals the worst side of the Reagan administration — the fact that it is quite willing to resort to force in circumstances where a) the evidence that a threat exists is minimal and b) the prospect of resistance is minuscule. Regrettably, that is also the definition of a bully. [203]

---

[200] M.T. Klare (1984) "Light Infantry Divisions: The 'In-Between' Deployment Force," *Nation*, Sept. 22, p. 240.
[201] Ibid.
[202] W.J. Olson (1985) "The Light Force Initiative," *Military Review*, vol. 65 (no. 6), p. 10.
[203] L. Aspin (1984) "A Look at the Grenada Invasion," *Congressional Record*, vol. 130 (no.1), p. E52.

The development and deployment of light infantry are consistent with this policy. The Bush administration's use of light infantry for the pre-Christmas surprise attack on Panama was consistent with this policy. The preparation of the 10th Mountain Light Infantry Division at Fort Drum and its potential use in Canada would also be consistent with this policy.

Propensities to engage in military actions would be aggravated if the United States were to have a major economic crisis, particularly if those actions served economic ends, were for the "benefit" of a close ally and replayed the Manifest Destiny themes of America's romanticized past. Also, because the US economy and political culture are structured on competitive, military preparation, the United States may become increasingly dangerous to its neighbors as communism and Russia weaken and the threat from that quarter diminishes. The United States is now searching for a suitable national enemy, but drug lords, Iraq, Libya, even Japan have been inadequate as national military missions.[204]

Compounding this danger is the fact that the Persian Gulf War has reduced or eliminated hesitancies and doubts in the United States about the use of military force as an instrument of foreign policy. William Olson, writing about light infantry strategies in 1985, questioned "whether the nation any longer has the will to use force, if necessary, to sustain US interests, especially when the rationale is not clear, immediate and overwhelming."[205] After Operation Desert Storm, the answer is affirmative. The one-sidedness of the victory and the passionate popular identification with that victory has indeed put the "Vietnam Syndrome" to rest. The US population may again have the will to use military force when the rationale for that force is not clear, or immediate, or overwhelming.

---

[204] A. Ferentzy . (1992) "Searching for an Enemy: Post-war America," *Our Times*, June, pp 19-21.
[205] W.J. Olson (1985) "The Light Force Initiative," *Military Review*, vol. 65 (no. 6), p. 4.

Canadians should take no comfort in arguments that threats to national sovereignty by the 10th Mountain Division at Fort Drum are unintentional. Intentions can be changed and rationalized very quickly, particularly for the "hair-trigger" troops now in place at Fort Drum. In defence planning, intentions should be judged by the facts of capability, not vice-versa. Fort Drum has all of the characteristics and capabilities of a force hostile to Canada.

CHAPTER 6

MODERN MANIFEST DESTINY

One need not presume that dangers to Canadian sovereignty are restricted to sinister conspiracies or to intentionally vicious designs specifically directed against Canadians. From a staid historical perspective, the threat may be spread more widely and more unconsciously throughout US political culture. "Manifest Destiny" is the belief that the United States has an inherent, natural and inevitable right to incorporate all of North America. This expansionist ideology has had a powerful continuity throughout US history.[206]

HISTORY

Canada was most clearly threatened by Manifest Destiny during the US War of Independence, the War of 1812 and the Oregon Crisis.[207]

---

[206] F. Merk (1963) *Manifest Destiny and Mission in American History: A Reinterpretation*, New York: Alfred Knopf.

A.K. Weinberg (1958) *Manifest Destiny: A Study of Nationalist Expansionism in American History*, Gloucester, MA: Peter Smith.

[207] R.C. Stuart (1988) *United States Expansionism and British North America, 1775-1871*, Chapel Hill, NC: University of North Carolina Press.

After the US Civil War, veterans of Irish descent organized themselves for military operations against Canada.[208] Their raids served to spur on Canadian confederation. In most people's minds, that was the extent of Manifest Destiny: an early nineteenth century phenomenon that died away more than 100 years ago. In the common perception, relations between Canada and the United States have long since matured to secure friendship and military alliance.

However, that is a misperception of history. Manifest Destiny has in fact continued to endanger Canada even as the two countries have moved in the direction of trust. Canadian historian Brian Cuthbertson observed:

The gradual change from enemies to allies was marked by an American reluctance to recognize the existence of another state with a different destiny on the North American continent and by the economic and military weakness of the new Dominion.[209]

In the late nineteenth century, in the early twentieth century, even now, one can observe in US political discourse the appeal to the goodness, the rightness and the inevitability of the United States assuming ownership of all of North America. For example, in 1887, US Secretary of State James G. Blaine proclaimed:

Canada is like an apple on a tree just beyond our reach. We may strive to grasp it, but the bough recedes from our hold just in proportion to our effort to catch it. Let it alone and in due time it will fall into our hands.[210]

In 1895, during a period of tensions between the United States and England, Theodore Roosevelt said that in a war with Great Britain, "Canada would surely be conquered ... and it would never be returned."[211] In 1911, speaking in support of the Taft-Laurier free

---

[208] M. Peterson. (1991) "Looking Back: The Fenian Raids," *Press-Republican* (Plattsburgh, NY), March 17, pp. C1-C2.
[209] B. Cuthbertson (1977) *Canadian Military Independence in the Age of the Superpowers*, Toronto: Fitzhenry and Whiteside, p. 1.
[210] C. Taylor (1977) *Six Journeys: A Canadian Pattern*, Toronto: Anansi, p. 10.
[211] H.F. Pringle (1939) *The Life and Times of William Howard Taft*, New York: Farrar and Rinehart, p. 589.

trade agreement, Congressman Champ Clark declared, "I hope to see the day when the American flag will float over every square foot of the British North American possessions clear to the North Pole."[212] President Taft's strategy to control the damage caused by this remark was to use ridicule:

The talk of annexation is bosh. Everyone who knows anything about it realizes that it is bosh ... and to make the possibility of the annexation of Canada by the United States a basis for objection to any steps toward their great economic and commercial union should be treated as one of the jokes of the platform.[213]

Ridicule has always been the preferred technique to dismiss concerns about US intrusions into Canada or plans for annexation.

In a 1923 visit to Vancouver, US President Harding again tried to assure Canadians that any ideas of annexation were long dead:

The great bugaboo of the United States scheming to annex Canada disappeared from all of our minds years and years ago ... And if I might be so bold as to offer a word of advice to you, it would be this: Do not encourage any enterprise looking to Canada's annexation of the United States. You are one of the most capable governing peoples of the world, but I entreat you, for your own sakes, to think twice before undertaking management of the territory which lies between the Great Lakes and the Rio Grande.[214]

Harding's jocular advice to abandon fears of annexation was apparently sincere, as was the Canadian applause. However, a contemporary Canadian review of that speech included the editorial response of the New York *Evening World*:

Yet the day must come when Canada will turn to the United States as an older brother and ask to come in. The North-West is largely American now, the French a menace to English-speaking control in the East.[215]

---

[212] Ibid.

[213] Ibid., p. 593.

[214] Anon. (1923) "Canadians Cheer Harding Assurance of Friendship," *New York Times*, July 27, pp. 1-2.

[215] G.M. Wrong (1923) "Relations with the United States," *Canadian Annual Review of Public Affairs*, vol. 23, pp. 51-84, quoting from p. 84.

FROM BALL TO BUCHANAN

Manifest Destiny is not dead and never has been. It still has considerable appeal and power in the United States, and it is still expressed by prominent political theorists in the United States. For example, George Ball, career foreign policy analyst and high State Department official during the Kennedy and Johnson administrations, argued that Canada must inevitably be pulled by natural forces and internal tensions into the passive, waiting arms of the United States. To resist is bad for Canadians and bad for the world:

Canada, I have long believed, is fighting a rearguard action against the inevitable. Living next to our nation, with a population ten times as large and a gross national product fourteen times as great, the Canadians recognize their need for United States capital, but at the same time they are determined to maintain their economic and political independence. Their position is understandable, and the desire to maintain their national integrity is a worthy objective. But the Canadians pay heavily for it and, over the years, I do not believe they will succeed in reconciling the intrinsic contradiction of their position. I wonder, for example, if the Canadian people will be prepared indefinitely to accept, for the psychic satisfaction of maintaining a separate national and political identity, a per capita income less than three-fourths of ours. The struggle is bound to be a difficult one — and I suspect, over the years, a losing one. Meanwhile there is danger that the efforts of successive Canadian governments to prevent United States economic domination will drive them toward increasingly restrictive nationalistic measures that are good neither for Canada nor for the health of the whole trading world.

Thus, while I can understand the motivating assumptions of the Canadian position, I cannot predict a long life expectancy for her present policies. The great land mass to the south exerts an enormous gravitational attraction while at the same time tending to repel, and even without the divisive element of a second culture in Quebec, the resultant strains and pressures are hard to endure. Sooner or later, commercial imperatives will bring about free movement of all goods back and forth across our long border, and when that occurs, or even before it does, it will become unmistakably clear that countries with economies so inextricably intertwined must also have free movement of the other vital factors of production — capital, services and labor. The result will

inevitably be substantial economic integration, which will require for its full realization a progressively expanding area of common political decision.[216]

This knowledge that economic union would lead to political union has motivated generations of Canadians, even to the present, to reject "free trade" arrangements with the United States. A summary review of recent public opinion polling concluded: "At no point since Gallup first posed this question to the public in the autumn of 1988 has a majority of the public backed the trade deal."[217] Ball's statement should also make Canadians wary of pronouncements and perceptions that the United States is totally passive in the pull of Canada into union.

A more recent expression of Manifest Destiny, still couched in passive language but displaying more eagerness, comes from Patrick Buchanan. He has been a White House advisor to Presidents Nixon, Ford, and Reagan.[218] He was a nationally syndicated newspaper and television columnist with a considerable public following. Buchanan was a flamboyant and outspoken candidate for the 1992 Republican presidential nomination, opening his campaign with a call for a "New Nationalism" to guard America against "the rise of a European super-state and a dynamic Asia led by Japan." [219]

In 1988, Buchanan wrote a newspaper column entitled, "Is Annexation of Canada in the Cards for the US?"[220] Buchanan cited Peter Brimelow's book, *The Patriot Game: Canada and the Canadian Question*, published by the rightwing Hoover Institution.[221] Brimelow is an expatriate Canadian who was once economic advisor to US Senator Orrin Hatch and who held editorial

[216] G.W. Ball (1968) *The Discipline of Power: Essentials of a Modern World Structure*, London: Bodley Head, p. 113.
[217] Anon. (1991) "Free Trade Opposition at Record High," *Toronto Star*, Nov. 4, p. A13.
[218] Anon. (1990) *Who's Who in America, 1990-91* (46th ed., vol. 1), Wilmette, IL: Macmillan.
[219] R. Turner (1992) "Buchanan, Urging New Nationalism, Joins '92 Race," *New York Times*, Dec. 11, p. B12.
[220] P. Buchanan (1988) "Is Annexation of Canada in the Cards for the US?" *The Bangor Daily News*, Jan. 19, p. 10.
[221] P. Brimelow (1986) *The Patriot Game: Canada and the Canadian Question*, Stanford, CA: Hoover Institution Press.

positions on *Barron's*, *Fortune*, and *Forbes*.[222] The argument is that French-English tensions in Canada will eventually lead to its breakup and incorporation by the United States. According to Buchanan, that would be good for Canadians. He quoted the famous US gangster, Al Capone, "I don't even know what street Canada is on," to encapsulate the attitude of most Americans to Canada, and then pointed out that the taking of Canada would be worthwhile and relatively easy:

But Americans would do well to pay attention to a neighbor with one-tenth our population, who possess as much of the earth's surface (6 percent) as does the United States.[223]

Another version of this column concluded that Quebec-style nationalism "is breaking out all over the globe" and "is the force of the future."[224]

Manifest Destiny is increasingly evident in US media, particularly expressions of it that ridicule Canadian sensibilities. Noam Chomsky once commented that if the United States ever were to invade Canada, the US propaganda system would probably drum up 90% support; in response, a comic song writer penned a song, "Let's Invade Canada."[225] Michael Kinsley, editor of the *New Republic*, entitled a column, "Let's do Canadians a Big Favor — and Annex Them."[226] This is a satirical essay, mocking Canadian fears about annexation, but at the same time making the case for it. In a similar vein, Joel Garreau wrote a satire, "Don't Cry for Canada — We'll Pick Up the Pieces."[227]

The theme that annexation is inevitable and a product of natural forces has not disappeared. Rather, it is being repeated in different forms. For example, nationally syndicated columnist Max Lerner

[222] Anon. (1991) *Who's Who in America, 1990-1991* (46th ed., vol. 1), Wilmette, IL: Macmillan.
[223] P. Buchanan (1988) "Is Annexation of Canada in the Cards for the US?" *The Bangor Daily News*, Jan. 19, p. 10.
[224] P. Buchanan (1988) "Can the Two Canadas Continue to Exist as One Nation?" *Chicago Sun-Times*, Jan. 20, p. 26.
[225] N. Chomsky (1991) Personal communication, April 27.
[226] M. Kinsley (1988) "Let's Do Canadians a Big Favor —and Annex Them," *Toronto Sunday Star*, Dec. 11, p. B3.
[227] J. Garreau (1990) "Don't Cry for Canada -We'll Pick Up the Pieces," *Washington Post*, June 17, pp. D1-D2.

wrote that there are two forces at work in the contemporary world, both of which are driving Canada into the American Union:

There is a double development taking place, worldwide. One is the thrust toward the breaking of federal systems under considerable tensions. The other toward federal integration when the time proves ripe for a sense of wholeness between nations too long apart.

History is moving the world not toward more fragments but toward ever-bigger functioning units. So I end with an invocation of my own. Look southward, Oh Canada. You may find there a working model, perhaps even someday a united North American home for you too.[228]

During the 1990 Meech Lake constitutional crisis, Buchanan repeated his annex-Canada theme several more times. In the *Washington Times*, he wrote:

A hard look at a map of Canada — as large as the United States, with but one tenth our population — suggests that, should the country come apart, America could pick up the pieces.[229]

In the *Los Angeles Times*, Buchanan clearly articulated for the American mind the appeal and hope that the annexation carries:

Observers have cried wolf about Canadian unity before, but this time the beast may be at hand ... We are living in historic times, when things are possible that many dreamed impossible in our lifetime.

The nations of Central Europe are breaking free, Germany is being reunited, the Russian Empire is dissolving ...

There is nothing wrong with Americans dreaming of a republic that, by the year 2000, encompasses the Atlantic and Western provinces of Canada, the Yukon and the Northwest Territories all the way to the Pole, and contains the world's largest island, Greenland (to be purchased from Denmark), giving the United States a land mass rivalling that of the Soviet Union, under a constitution providing all of its people freedom to realize all their dreams.

The twenty-first century then, could not but be the Second American Century.[230]

Buchanan's column entitled "Fluttering Maple Leaves" provoked a response from Canada's ambassador to the United States. He

---

[228] M. Lerner (1990) "Max Lerner on Federations," *Whig-Standard*, July 28, p. 8.

[229] J. Valorzi (1990) "Separatism Inevitable Columnists in US Say," *Whig-Standard*, April 17, p. 14.

[230] P. Buchanan (1990), excerpted as, "Canadian Disunity and the Rise of the American Empire," *Globe and Mail*, April 17, p. A7.

called Buchanan's ideas "contemporary versions of Manifest Destiny."[231] Columnist William Schneider of the *Los Angeles Times* has similarly rebuked the chorus of conservative columnists applauding the impending break-up of Canada.[232]

AMERICAN RENAISSANCE

The most comprehensive and enrapturing contemporary statement of Manifest Destiny appears in the book *American Renaissance*, by Marvin Cetron and Owen Davies. This book purports to show how all of the present problems that beset the United States and threaten its power and standard of living will be resolved by the turn of the century. Unemployment, crime, drugs, trade imbalance, AIDS, inflation, cancer, terrorism, racial tensions — everything — will come out all right. The book's Manifesto reads:

American Renaissance **is a statement of hope. We believe firmly that anyone who looks clearly at the facts, unbiased by any partisan political agenda, must feel an unfashionable optimism about the future of our country. In the decade to come, America will begin to solve many of the problems that have dogged it for so long.[233]**

One of the major keys to this turnaround is the annexation of Canada by the United States. The chapter, "The Struggle for Economic Supremacy," opens with the question, "Can the United States still compete effectively with other nations in the years ahead?", which is immediately answered: "... the United States *must* be able to compete in order to maintain the standard of living to which most Americans have become accustomed."[234] After accounting for the competition of Japan, East Asia and the New Europe, the discussion of "The American Bloc" begins:

---

[231] Anon. (1990) "US Writer Reasserts Separatism for Quebec," *Whig-Standard*, May 3, p. 8.
[232] Anon. (1990) "William Schneider on English Canadians," *Whig-Standard*, July 31, p. 6.
[233] M. Cetron and O. Davies (1989) *American Renaissance: Our Life at the Turn of the 21st Century*, New York: St.Martin's Press, p. 7.
[234] Ibid., p. 213.

One of the most important factors in America's future prosperity was decided not in Washington, but north of our border. When Canada's voters went to the polls in November 1988 to elect a Prime Minister, the decisive issue in their minds was the historic free-trade agreement with the United States.[235]

The authors fail to note that a majority of Canadians voted against free trade. The authors describe regionalism and Quebec separatism as positive and inevitable. The scenario continues:

Once the free-trade agreement with the United States takes full effect, the next logical step will be to accept politically what has already happened economically — the integration of Canada into the United States ... In fact, incorporating most of Canada into the United States will do neither nation much good beyond, perhaps, the psychological benefit of recognizing reality. The 1988 free-trade agreement will accomplish far more. Though Canada's population represents a relatively small market compared to Japan, France, or Germany, the guarantee of unrestricted access to both Canada's people and its raw materials will give American manufacturers a safe haven from which to support their other trading ventures.[236]

Cetron and Davies have continued this argument in their new book, *Crystal Globe*.[237] They conclude that "English-speaking Canada will opt to join the United States within the next ten years."[238] To press the point with a bit of ridicule, the chapter on the Soviet Union is entitled, "Soviet Confederation: A Canada with 15 Quebecs."

George Ball, Patrick Buchanan, Michael Kinsley — these are not minor figures in US political culture. They, and other nationalists like them who have been applauding the political and economic crises in Canada, are not without influence on US policies and plans. They couch their ideas in terms of natural forces, the "luck of the cards" and historic Canadian tensions. They present the United States as a passive bystander. But it is only realistic to expect that they would be influencing US planning in order to fulfill the vision that so entices them. What steps might be taken to

---

[235] Ibid., p. 221.
[236] Ibid., pp. 223-224.
[237] M. Cetron and O. Davies (1991) *Crystal Globe: The Have and Have-Nots of the New World Order*, New York: St.Martin's Press.
[238] Ibid., p. 91.

secure a prize upon which rests hope of continuing US economic power and dominance?

It is easy to speculate that natural Canadian tendencies toward disunity and disorder might be helped along, discreetly, covertly. There can be no doubt that Canadian political passions, including regionalism, French nationalism, anti-bilingualism and Native self-rule, are all genuine. But US contributions to inflaming those passions should not be ruled out, whether in the form of public applause, covert funding, agents provocateurs, or compromised politicians. For example, during the Oka Crisis, some Mohawks claimed that there was external manipulation of the event. Mohawk lawyer Frank Horn said that he believes that the Mohawk Warriors were being paid by an unknown source: "Nobody knows who we're dealing with. Who is benefitting? Somebody is benefitting." He added that whoever is "stirring it up" should be exposed.[239] The conditions for conflict were ripe and the consequences of "stirring it up" were predictable.[240] Who benefits from distrust and violence between native people and French Quebeckers? What plans might have been advanced by the Oka Crisis? If political forces in the United States are hoping for conflict and conflagration in Canada, if they are striking sparks, then it is reasonable they might prepare forces to help put out the fire. All-weather, rapid-deployment assault forces ready and waiting at the border would be suitable.

---

[239] A. Bailey (1990) "Separatism Scares Natives, Mohawk Says," *Whig-Standard*, July 18, p. 1.

[240] S. Conterta (1992) "Native Deal Stirs Deep Fears In Quebec," *Toronto Star*, July 19, p. A10.

CHAPTER 7

DECADES OF PLANNING WAR ON CANADA

The idea that Fort Drum may represent US military preparations for contingencies in Canada is not credible to many people because they turn their mind's eye to recent history and see only a long period of peaceful relations and military alliance. Canada and the United States were allies in World War I, World War II, the Korean War, the Cold War and the Persian Gulf War. There has been a longstanding agreement, people believe, to demilitarize the border. There are mutual defence arrangements in NATO and NORAD. Most people would acknowledge an active US threat to Canada in the early nineteenth century, but laugh at that possibility in the present. However, this easy dismissal of concern becomes less confident as US military designs against Canada in recent history are exposed.

A RECORD OF DUPLICITY

The fact is, the United States has a long record of covert peacetime planning for war against Canada. This has been well documented by Richard Preston in his book *The Defence of the Undefended*

Border.[241] His research is based on index records to war plans at the US Army War College, on period military journals and on materials retrieved from US archives. The orthodox textbook history has it that treaties and traditions effectively demilitarized the US-Canada border more than a century ago. The fact is, however, that the border has never been demilitarized. The Rush-Bagot Agreement of 1817, so often cited as a disarmament document, only specified the numbers and sizes of warships in border waters. The Treaty of Washington in 1871 settled all outstanding disputes between the United States and Canada, but it was not a document of demilitarization. The British presumed that the treaty ended concern about war in North America and began military withdrawal from the continent.[242] The United States did allow many border fortifications and military facilities to lapse into disrepair, but US strategic planners have never been at peace with a border on the north. They never did give up plans and preparations for war against Canada. Even in the least threatening of times, in fact, especially at those times, the US military maintained an obsessive fixation on military campaigns along their northern border. Considering the economic and demographic imbalances of the two nations, US military planning against Canada has been aggressive rather than defensive.

The modern history of US military planning against Canada begins with the Treaty of Washington in 1871 when the British military left North America. In 1878, a US war plan was prepared, entitled, "The Military Resources of Canada: Plan of Invasion."[243] In 1881, the US Secretary of War reported to the Senate that Fort Montgomery, 64 kilometers (40 miles) south of Montreal, should be maintained:

---

[241] R.A. Preston (1977) *The Defence of the Undefended Border: Planning for War in North America 1867-1939*, Montreal: McGill-Queen's University Press.
[242] Ibid, p. 60.
[243] Ibid., p. 93.

... for an invasion of Canada on this line of operations it would at once be a fortified base and store-house for the invading army.[244]

Fort Montgomery is known locally as Fort Blunder because it was mistakenly built by the United States on the Canadian side of the border.[245] In 1882, another plan of invasion was prepared, even though war seemed an unlikely possibility.[246] In 1888, the *Journal of the Military Service Institutions of the United States* featured an article arguing that fishing disputes between Canada and the United States might lead to war, which would require "invading the Dominion to seize Windsor, Fort Erie, Prescott and the four bridges over the Niagara River."[247] Prescott faces Ogdensburg, New York, about 50 kilometers (32 miles) from Fort Drum. Winnipeg, too, was to be taken to sever transportation to the west. However, it was argued that peaceful annexation of Canada was the preferred option. The *New York World* the same year published a map of the United States after the annexation of Canada.[248]

Some people would dismiss these war plans as private intellectual exercises by military officers made idle by peace. But coincident with these plans was a program of military espionage directed at Canada. For example, in 1880 US Adjutant-General R.C. Drum ordered all officers travelling in foreign countries to gather military intelligence and then also ordered border base commanders to facilitate leaves of absence for officers to take cross-border hunting holidays.[249] These orders were confirmed and strengthened in 1881 and 1884. In 1885, the Information Division of the War Department was established to gather military intelligence in

---

[244] Ibid., p. 85.
[245] Anon. (1915) "With Blue and Red," *Plattsburgh Daily Press*, Aug. 30, p.3.
[246] R.A. Preston (1977) *The Defence of the Undefended Border: Planning for War in North America 1867-1939*, Montreal: McGill-Queen's University Press, p. 93.
[247] Ibid., p. 104.
[248] Ibid., reproduction on p. 106.
[249] Ibid., p. 92.

expectation of war over east coast fishing disputes with Canada.[250] The new intelligence service was specifically charged to gather information about the northern frontier.[251] In 1886, the United States Army prepared another analysis of Canadian military resources and another invasion plan.[252] In 1887, confidential orders were given for reconnaissance patrols into Canada. By 1889, the flow of information was so great that a special section of the adjutant-general's office was set up to receive it. The same year saw more detailed plans for invasion.[253] In 1890, the US Naval Secret Strategy Board prepared plans for war against Canada.[254] During this period, Canada had no comparable planning or preparation.

In 1891, Madison Barracks at Sackets Harbor near present-day Fort Drum was selected as one of the "important military stations" on the border, to quote from the *Army and Navy Journal.*[255] On the other side of the border, that same year, the Canadian Army departed Fort Henry in Kingston. In 1892, Major-General Oliver Howard in command of the Eastern Division prepared plans for the conquest of Canada.[256] In the same year, US military forces on the border were trebled, and the US adjutant-general requested new plans for war against Canada.[257] In 1893, when Congress was opposed to further military preparations at the border in "an age of peace" when "the Canadians are our friends," a new military base for cavalry was built in Burlington, Vermont, south of Montreal. In 1893, US Major-General Nelson Miles presented the invasion

---

[250] Ibid., p. 103.
    H. Wrong (1976) "Two Centuries in the Shadow of the Behemoth: The Effect on the Canadian Psyche," *International Journal,* vol. 31 (no. 3), pp. 413-433.
[251] R.A. Preston (1977) *The Defence of the Undefended Border: Planning for War in North America 1867-1939,* Montreal: McGill-Queen's University Press, p. 103.
[252] Ibid., p. 110.
[253] Ibid., p. 111.
[254] Ibid., p. 122.
[255] Ibid., p. 117.
[256] Ibid., p. 122.
[257] Ibid., pp. 117 and 122.

plans requested by the adjutant general. He recommended a sudden winter offensive to capture Montreal and Ottawa and also planned that a spring offensive should cross the St. Lawrence River and capture the Rideau canal system. Other targets were Winnipeg and Vancouver. [258]

In 1895, US President Cleveland invoked the Monroe Doctrine to threaten war against Britain because of Venezuela's border dispute with British Guiana.[259] This is what prompted Theodore Roosevelt's proclamation that in the event of such a war, Canada would be conquered and annexed.[260] In fact, several months earlier, the US Naval War College outlined a plan for the invasion of Canada. Then, in 1896, the Secretary of the Navy ordered Commodore Charles Gridley to prepare detailed plans for war with Canada. This was to be done in strictest secrecy, to allow surprise on the Canadians, to avoid public outcry over breach of the Rush-Bagot Agreement and perhaps even to keep President Cleveland ignorant of the preparations.[261] Gridley did extensive reconnaissance on both sides of the border and found ample evidence that Canada was quite unprepared for war. He recommended that a US invasion force cross the St. Lawrence River below Ogdensburg, New York, near the present site of Fort Drum, in order to quickly cut Canada's east-west shipping and rail lines. It was later revealed by the former US Secretary of War that this was to have been a surprise attack done simultaneously with a declaration of war, exactly in the style of the Japanese surprise attack on Pearl Harbour.[262] US planning for war did not disrupt the surface of good relations between Canadian and US military personnel. For example, in February 1896, Canadian

---

[258] Ibid., p. 122.
[259] Ibid., p. 124.
[260] H.F. Pringle (1939) The Life and Times of William Howard Taft, New York: Farrar and Rinehart, p. 589.
[261] R.A. Preston (1977) The Defence of the Undefended Border: Planning for War in North America 1867-1939, Montreal: McGill-Queen's University Press, pp. 134-135.
[262] Ibid., p. 152.

militia officers from Kingston were hosted at a reception at Madison Barracks in Sackets Harbor.[263]

Preston's concluding analysis of this episode focused on the anti-democratic, subservsive nature of US military planning:

American planning for war at the time of the Venezuela crisis had thus gone much further than that of Britain and Canada, and it aimed at anticipatory action, or preemptive strike, to forestall a long war that the United States would win in the end only if the American public remained steadfast. Secrecy had been necessary because, although a British attack might have consolidated American opinion in defence of the country, the knowledge that American officers had planned the first blow might possibly have been divisive in the United States and might have destroyed the essential patriotic unity required for prosecuting the war.[264]

In 1897, gold was discovered in the Yukon, and the exact boundary between Canada and the US territory of Alaska became an issue. Theodore Roosevelt was to make some hint of taking his "big stick" to Canada, but the dispute was referred to arbitration and eventually settled. Furthermore, the Spanish-American War diverted US military attention away from the north, and Britain was seen as a friend of the United States for backing the conquests of Cuba and the Philippines.[265] It was a period of friendship and peaceful commerce between Canada and the United States. In 1898, the international bridge was built across the St. Lawrence River at Cornwall.

ORIGINS OF FORT DRUM

In 1903, the Army War College was created as the US Army's only planning agency. That same year it received a *Plan of General Wood — Invasion of Canada*.[266] Brigadier-General Leonard Wood was a former military governor of Cuba and a future Chief of Staff of the US

---

[263] Ibid., pp. 130-131.
[264] Ibid., p. 135.
[265] Ibid., pp. 150-151.
[266] Ibid., pp. 150-151.

Army. Following Wood's plan, maps of Canada were collected. In 1904, the War College "filed information for use in the preparation of a plan for the invasion of Canada."[267] That same year, the Joint Board of the Army and Navy was formed and the tradition of color coding countries for war plans was begun.[268] In 1905, British military intelligence learned that "American commanders along the border had been ordered to study the terrain and to report to the chief of staff on plans for mobilization and concentration for an invasion of Canada."[269] Special US reconnaissances were being made into Canada. This is the context of the beginning of Fort Drum.

In 1901, Theodore Roosevelt became President of the United States. This is the same Roosevelt who had threatened war on Canada during the Venezuela Crisis and during the Alaska boundary dispute. As President, he advocated that the Army should establish camps for large scale summer maneuvers.[270] One of these camps was to be in New York State. Sites were being considered near Albany, in the Adirondack Mountains and on Long Island. Border sites at the remote northern tier of the state were not thought to be likely candidates. The *New York Times* reported in 1906:

Plattsburgh Barracks have also been recommended, as has also a strip of land known as Pine Plains [now Fort Drum] near Watertown. It is not thought that either of these places will be selected.[271]

The summer exercises were for joint mobilization maneuvres of regular Army and militia forces coming largely from New England and the mid-Atlantic states of New Jersey, Pennsylvania and Maryland.[272] This was undoubtedly part of a strategic reorganization

---

[267] Ibid., p. 164.
[268] Ibid., p. 165.
[269] Ibid., p. 160.
[270] Anon. (1906) "Army to Concentrate in Six Great Camps," *New York Times*, May 15, p. 2.
[271] Ibid.
[272] Anon. (1908) *Encampment of United States Army and National Guard, Military Department of the East, at Pine Camp, Jefferson County, N.Y., June 15 to July 15, 1908*, Watertown, NY: Hungerford-Holbrook.

of the Army in order to be able to raise a 400,000 man force on short notice.[273] Pines Plains, while far from central for these units, was selected as the site. Curiously, one US Army document dates the origin of Pine Camp to be 1906.[274] This is possibly an error, possibly a reference to the true Army decision to put a base at the present site of Fort Drum, three years in advance of the official decision.

Field officers disapproved of Pine Camp as a training ground,[275] and on the first day of encampment a sudden violent storm destroyed the headquarters, stampeded the horses, blew away the payroll and caused maneuvres to be suspended.[276] Nevertheless, Secretary of War R.S. Oliver arrived a few days later, declared the maneuvres a success and announced that the site would be purchased as the eventual training ground for the mobilization of 50,000 troops.[277] He said that "so perfectly and so thoroughly worked out are the plans of the department" that they would go ahead even if he were to leave office. He said that space for expansion was an attractive point. This is in direct contradiction to the judgement of the panel of six Army officers formally appointed by the War Department to evaluate the plan to purchase Pine Plains. The panel recommended against Pine Plains because of lack of training space, inadequate transportation and bad weather.[278] As with the recent decision to expand Fort Drum, it seems a prior decision was going ahead no matter what objections came forth.

The most important point in this history, not mentioned in the official version, is that the historical first use of Fort Drum was to

[273] Anon. (1906) "Big Army on Short Notice," New York Times, January 21, p. 3.
[274] M.S. Sowell (1978) Environment Impact Statement Concerning the Restationing of Troops Redeploying from Korea. Mobile, Alabama: US Army Corps of Engineers.
[275] Anon. (1908) "50,000 Men May Camp at the Plains," Watertown Daily Times, June 23, p. 8.
[276] Anon. (1908) "$25,000 of Army Pay Scattered by Wind," New York Times, June 15, p. 1.
    Anon. (1908) "Big Army Camp Busy Drying Out," Watertown Daily Times, June 16, p. 11.
[277] Anon. (1908) "50,000 Men May Camp at the Plains," Watertown Daily Times, June 23, p. 8.
[278] Anon. (1908) "Oppose Pine Plains as Maneuvre Site," New York Times, July 27, p. 3.

practise for war against Canada. The script for the 1908 maneuvres presumed that US forces are mustering at Ogdensburgh presumably preparing to invade Canada at the long identified point of best-crossing. They are outflanked by a Canadian force crossing at the Thousand Islands:

A Blue army (imaginary) is retreating south from Ogdensburg to prevent being cut off by a superior invading Brown army (imaginary) which has crossed from Kingston to Clayton.[279]

This was the scenario even though the British army had left Kingston in 1870 and Canadian regulars had left in 1891. US military intelligence knew that Canadian militia were quite unprepared for war.[280] The war game script called for US Blue forces to win when superior numbers eventually reach the field.[281]

The land was purchased in 1909 and named Pine Camp. There was some concern that the $75,000 purchase price was too expensive.[282] The similarities of these 1908-1909 events to the recent expansion at Fort Drum are remarkable: advanced decisions are made to look post-hoc, bad weather, bad location, bad transportation and high costs are brushed aside, and the judgements of the Army's own formal decision panels are overruled.

According to Preston's sources, planning for war against Canada "got into full swing" in 1908 and 1909.[283] In 1909, Captain Lucien Dade of the 13th Cavalry, which trained at Pine Camp the previous year,[284] stressed the importance of a rapid seizure of the St.

---

[279] Anon. (1908) "Forces Cross from Kingston to Clayton," *Watertown Daily Times,* June 19, p. 8.

[280] R.A. Preston (1977) *The Defence of the Undefended Border: Planning for War in North America 1867-1939,* Montreal: McGill-Queen's University Press.

[281] Anon. (1908) "Army Besieges Watertown," *Watertown Daily Times,* July 1, p. 4.

[282] Anon. (1909) "Oliver Strongly Urges the Site," *Watertown Daily Times,* Feb. 5, p. 4.
Anon. (1974) "Pine Plains, Pine Camp, Camp Drum, Fort Drum," *Town and Country* (Watertown), October 3, 1974.

[283] R.A. Preston (1977) *The Defence of the Undefended Border: Planning for War in North America 1867-1939,* Montreal: McGill-Queen's University Press, p. 188.

[284] Anon. (1908) *Encampment of United States Army and National Guard, Military Department of the East, at Pine Camp, Jefferson County, N.Y., June 15 to July 15, 1908,* Watertown, NY: Hungerford-Holbrook.

Lawrence canals in the event of war against Canada.[285] Major David Jewitt Baker, of the 11th Cavalry, which had also trained at Pine Camp the previous year,[286] prepared an invasion plan aimed at the capture of Montreal and Quebec City.[287] A more detailed invasion plan the following year argued that trade disputes with Canada were a likely cause of war and emphasized "control of the St. Lawrence route by building a fort on the New York bank of the river."[288] The plan developed at the War College in 1911 focused on attacking Winnipeg and cutting Canadian rail lines.[289] This is the year of the Taft-Laurier free trade agreement.[290] This is the year that President Taft said that "talk of annexation is bosh," a "joke," and is no cause for rejecting free trade.[291]

The 1910 war games were again at Pine Camp, playing out the Blue (US) vs. Red (Britain and Canada) war plan scenario that was to become standard for the next three decades.[292] As usual, bad weather — "a forty-mile wind, a drenching rain, and a winter temperature" — disrupted the maneuvres and caused them to be cancelled.[293] The *New York Sun*, through surmise or through a leak of strategic war plan information, headlined a report "Canadian Army Crushed."[294] This happened even though prior press releases had identified the code "Blue" to mean "North" and "Red" to

[285] R.A. Preston (1977) *The Defence of the Undefended Border: Planning for War in North America 1867-1939*, Montreal: McGill-Queen's University Press, p. 188.

[286] Anon. (1908) *Encampment of United States Army and National Guard, Military Department of the East, at Pine Camp, Jefferson County, N.Y., June 15 to July 15, 1908*, Watertown, NY: Hungerford-Holbrook.

[287] R.A. Preston (1977) *The Defence of the Undefended Border: Planning for War in North America 1867-1939*, Montreal: McGill-Queen's University Press, p. 188.

[288] Ibid.

[289] Ibid., p. 189.

[290] E. Kierans and W. Stewart (1988) *Wrong End of the Rainbow: The Collapse of Free Enterprise in Canada*, Toronto: Collins.

[291] H.F. Pringle (1939) *The Life and Times of William Howard Taft*, New York: Farrar and Rinehart, p. 593.

[292] Anon. (1910) "Blue Crush Red in Practice Fight," *New York Times*, August 2, p. 6.

[293] Anon. (1910) "Squadron A 'Dead' Dined by Grant: Icy Blast Stops Battle," *New York Times*, August 6, p. 4.

[294] Anon. (1910) "Common Sense Vs. Peace Fustian ," *United States Army and Navy Journal and Gazette*, vol. 45, October 15, pp. 184-185.

mean "South."[295] The *US Army and Navy Journal* explained that the *New York Sun* was just joking and that the war plan never actually mentioned the word "Canada."[296] The 1911 summer maneuvres were a sudden mobilization of 20,000 troops and two naval fleets to the Mexican border.[297] These were declared to be routine war games, but within a few days, it was made clear by President Taft that these were invasion forces.[298]

Planning for war against Canada continued apace. In 1912, War College documents emphasized that "Kingston was the most strategic point" in Canada and that the best place for American invasion forces to cross the St. Lawrence was at Cornwall, about 115 kilometers (70 miles) from present-day Fort Drum.[299] The plan was to destroy the Rideau Canal and to march on Ottawa. At the same time this planning was going on, the budget managers in the War Department recommended closing several military bases, including Madison Barracks at Sackets Harbor, Plattsburgh Barracks, and Fort Ethan Allen in Burlington, Vermont.[300] As in 1991, surplus bases bordering on central Canada were not closed.

Lieutenant-Colonel Thomas B. Dugan's 1912 *Military Geography of the Provinces of Ontario and Quebec, to Include a Study of an Attack on those Provinces by the United States* noted that Canadian militia were ill-prepared for war with poor training and too-frequent absences without leave.[301] The proposal was made that US forces cross the St. Lawrence River by a pontoon bridge and a

---

[295] Anon. (1910) "Squadron A Saved from Annihilation," *New York Times*, August 5, p. 5.

[296] Anon. (1910) "Common Sense Vs. Peace Fustian ," *United States Army and Navy Journal and Gazette*, vol. 45, October 15, pp. 184-185.

[297] Anon. (1911) "20,000 Troops and Two Naval Divisions to Mobilize Near Mexican Border," *New York Times*, March 8, pp. 1-2.

[298] Anon. (1911) "Taft to Stop Aid to Rebels and End Revolt," *New York Times*, March 10, p. 1.

[299] R.A. Preston (1977) *The Defence of the Undefended Border: Planning for War in North America 1867-1939*, Montreal: McGill-Queen's University Press, p. 190.

[300] Ibid., p. 197.

[301] Ibid., p. 271.

recommendation was made that there should be an exhaustive reconnaissance of the river to determine a best crossing point. In fact, a military mapping of northern New York shorelines was undertaken in 1913.[302] Others at the War College prepared a detailed plan for an invasion force to cross at Cornwall from a staging area at Moira, New York, northwest of present-day Fort Drum. This plan was labelled "Invasion of Canada (Canadian War Plan)" and was filed for future use.[303] War College documents from 1913 argued that war with Britain would be improbable, that the United States would not be the aggressor, but that plans must be made to move the war as quickly as possible to Canadian territory.[304] Lieutenant-Colonel B.H. Fuller's 1914 "Military Geography of Eastern Canada and a Study of an Invasion by United States Forces" again emphasized the importance of Kingston and that Canada would be easy to conquer.[305]

EVEN AFTER WWI

During all of this period, Canada thought itself on friendly and peaceful terms with the United States and had no comparable military planning, espionage, or preparation. Nevertheless, on the US side, offensive military planning against Canada continued even as Canada and England entered World War I and were busy fighting German aggression in Europe. For example, in 1915, Brigadier-General M.M. Macomb sent detailed operational plans for the invasion of Canada for approval by the chief of staff of the US Army.[306] The 1915 summer maneuvres were held at Plattsburgh, with the scenario of a Red army from Canada being defeated by the

---

[302] Anon. (1913) "Lieut. French, Third Army at Fort Ontario, Mapping Northern N.Y.," *Watertown Daily Times*, Aug. 11, p. 9.
[303] R.A. Preston (1977) *The Defence of the Undefended Border: Planning for War in North America 1867-1939*, Montreal: McGill-Queen's University Press, pp. 191, 271.
[304] Ibid., p. 191.
[305] Ibid., pp. 191, 272.
[306] Ibid., p. 192.

Blue army in a final battle at Fort Montgomery right on the Canadian border.[307] The 1916 War College plans, culminating nine years of secret planning to conquer Canada, included a map showing the Fourth Division mustering at Madison Barracks near the present Fort Drum. [308] That force was to cross the St. Lawrence, seize Kingston, and then contribute to the capture of Ottawa and Montreal.

US entry into World War I caused a break in planning for war against Canada. But in 1919 the US Joint Board of the army and navy was revived, as was war planning against Canada.[309] In 1919, military intelligence operations against Canada were in full operation, although on-site reconnaissance missions into Canada were explicitly forbidden since they might attract attention.[310] The US Army devised a battle plan for the seizure of Saskatchewan using cavalry, tanks and railway cannon.[311] The 1921 War College documents emphasized, again, the need for a US invasion of Canada to begin by crossing the St. Lawrence River in order to cut east-west transportation routes.[312] On the Canadian side, Colonel Sutherland-Brown's *Defence Scheme #1* was prepared in 1921, apparently in complete ignorance of actual US military planning to invade Canada.[313]

In 1923, US President Harding came to Vancouver to say, "The great bugaboo of the United States scheming to annex Canada

[307] Anon. (1915) "Plattsburgh Army Begins War Games," *New York Times*, August 28, p. 14.
Anon. (1915) "Recruits Defeat the Red Invaders: Blue Army Wins Battle of Fort Montgomery on the Canadian Border," *New York Times*, August 31, p. 4.
[308] R.A. Preston (1977) *The Defence of the Undefended Border: Planning for War in North America 1867-1939*, Montreal: McGill-Queen's University Press, pp. 193-194.
[309] Ibid., pp. 220-221.
[310] Ibid., pp. 220, 223.
[311] C. Taylor (1977) *Six Journeys: A Canadian Pattern*, Toronto: Anansi, p. 24.
[312] R.A. Preston (1977) *The Defence of the Undefended Border: Planning for War in North America 1867-1939*, Montreal: McGill-Queen's University Press, p. 220.
[313] Ibid, pp. 215-217.

disappeared from all of our minds years and years ago ..."[314] In 1924, *Army Strategic Plan Red* detailed the conquest and occupation of Canada by four armies and concluded:

Blue intentions are to hold in perpetuity all Crimson (Canadian) and Red (British) territories gained. The policy will be to prepare provinces and territories of Crimson and Red to become states and territories of the Blue Union upon the declaration of peace. The Dominion government will be abolished ... [315]

In 1925, the Operations Division of the General Staff began efforts to perfect *Army Strategic Plan Red*.[316] In 1926, the International Peace Bridge was built between Buffalo and Fort Erie. The 1928 draft of *Strategic Plan Red* argued that "it should be made quite clear to Canada that in a war she would suffer grievously." [317] That same year a military airfield was established at Pine Camp.[318] In 1929, the *War Plan Red* was tentatively approved and given to the War Department for mobilization planning. This all continued apace despite US intelligence reports that Canada was in a very non-military posture. For example, in 1930, the US Naval Attaché in Ottawa reported:

In as much as Canada had no idea of trouble with any other country it was not considered necessary to maintain a proper air force. [319]

---

[314] Anon. (1923) "Canadians Cheer Harding Assurance of Friendship," *New York Times*, July 27, pp. 1-2.
[315] R.A. Preston (1977) *The Defence of the Undefended Border: Planning for War in North America 1867-1939*, Montreal: McGill-Queen's University Press, p. 221.
[316] Ibid.
[317] Ibid., p. 223.
[318] Anon. (1928) "Pine Camp Field Dedicated," *New York Times*, July 14, p. 13.
[319] Anon. (1930) "US Naval Intelligence Dept. Attaché's Report: Royal Canadian Air Force," Dec. 20, 1930, US Naval War College Records, ser. no. 863, cited by R.A. Preston (1977) *The Defence of the Undefended Border: Planning for War in North America 1867-1939*, Montreal: McGill-Queen's University Press, pp. 222, 277.

CHAPTER 8

WAR PLAN RED

Most of these early US plans to attack Canada are now known only through index entries and by mentions in memoranda. However, the culmination of these plans — three decades in secret development — is available in US archives. *War Plan Red* was approved as official US military policy on May 10, 1930, by the Secretary of the Navy and the acting Secretary of War.[320] *War Plan Red* was declassified in 1974[321] and was reported immediately in the *Canadian Defence Quarterly*[322] as a postscript to a previous article on Canada's 1920s military plans for defence against the United States.[323] Preston gives only a few pages to *War Plan Red* in his 1977

---

[320] R.A. Preston (1977) *The Defence of the Undefended Border: Planning for War in North America 1867-1939*, Montreal: McGill-Queen's University Press, p. 223.

[321] In the following discussion, *War Plan Red* refers to *Joint Army and Navy Basic War Plan - Red*, microfilm, Roll #10, J.B. 325, Serial 435 through Serial 641, obtained from the the US National Archives in Washington D.C. on November 12, 1991.

[322] R.A. Preston (1974) "Buster Brown was not Alone — A Postscript," *Canadian Defence Quarterly*, vol. 4 (no. 1), pp. 11-12.

[323] R.A. Preston (1974) "Buster Brown was not Alone: American Plans for the Invasion of Canada, 1919-1939," *Canadian Defence Quarterly*, vol. 3 (no. 4), pp. 47-58.

book.[324] There is an extended discussion in a recent but little distributed military history journal.[325] Other than that, there appears to have been little reference to, or discussion of, *War Plan Red*, even though it is the only fully-developed, detailed, and available plan by a foreign nation for the conquest of Canada. Canada's Royal Military College did not have a copy until it was provided by the author of this book. *War Plan Red* became more widely known when the Syracuse *Post-Standard* reported it in March 1991 and suggested that the unusual preparations at Fort Drum are consistent with those earlier attack plans.[326]

War Plan Red presumed that US efforts to become more competitive in global markets during hard economic times would lead to conflict with Great Britain and to the opportunity to conquer Canada. The plan called for US naval and army forces to prepare for rapid coordinated attacks on key Canadian cities. The primary targets of attack were Halifax, Montreal and Quebec, but the Niagara region, Sault Ste. Marie, Winnipeg and Vancouver were also identified as strategically important.

CONQUEST OF CANADA

The most curious aspect of *War Plan Red* is something that does not appear: the word "Canada." To invoke the objective, analytic air of a rational contingency plan, the nations involved are colour coded: BLUE stands for the United States, RED stands for the United Kingdom, CRIMSON stands for Canada, SCARLET stands for Australia, ORANGE stands for Japan, and GREEN

---

[324] R.A. Preston (1977) *The Defence of the Undefended Border: Planning for War in North America 1867-1939*, Montreal: McGill-Queen's University Press.

[325] T. Holt (1988). "Joint Plan Red," *MHQ: The Quarterly Journal of Military History*, vol. 1 (no. 1), pp. 48-55.

[326] J.D. Salant (1991) "The War that Never Was," *Post-Standard* (Syracuse), March 25, pp. A1, A4.

   P. Peirol (1991) "US Plan to Attack Canada in 1930 Causes Stir," *Whig-Standard*, March 27, pp. 1-2.

   D. Pugliese (1991) "Invasion 1930: US had Plan to Attack Canada to Win Economic Battle with Britain," *Ottawa Citizen*, March 27, pp. A1-A2.

stands for Mexico. Although the plan is about a war between RED and BLUE, most of the document is about the conquest of CRIMSON. The words "United Kingdom" and "United States" appear frequently in the text, but the word "Canada" is absent. Only embedded in lists of RED resources is the adjective "Canadian" used — only twice in the whole document.[327] Many other countries are named in the text — Ireland, Japan, Argentina, the Philippines — but not Canada. Canadian cities are identified by name — Cornwall, Sudbury, Moncton, Victoria, Kingston — but not Canada. Even Canadian provinces are named — Quebec, Nova Scotia, Ontario, British Columbia. One needs to know geography to know that CRIMSON is Canada:

CRIMSON is defined as all of RED territory located north of the northern part of the United States.[328]

It is as though there is a taboo against naming the victim, or perhaps some need to deny the existence of what is to be extinguished. Canada had been an independent self-governing country since 1867. Or, perhaps, this is an early example of planned deniability. If War Plan Red were to become public, US officials could deny, as they did in 1910, that there is any mention of "Canada" in the document.

A second curious omission is the lack of any discussion of contingencies for the military occupation of Canada. There is no explicit statement of what is to become of conquered CRIMSON. The Theatre of Operations for the US Army is defined to be "All CRIMSON territory."[329] The mission is declared in bold type:

ULTIMATELY, TO GAIN COMPLETE CONTROL OF CRIMSON. The execution of this decision will require: By the Army — extension of operations to include all CRIMSON vital areas not occupied by the initial operations ...[330]

---

[327] *War Plan Red,* pp. 15, 16.
[328] Ibid., p. 79.
[329] Ibid., p. 80.
[330] Ibid., p. 84.

Is the foreseeable end of this whole conflict the perpetual military occupation of CRIMSON? Or the eventual "return" of CRIMSON to independence? Or perhaps the annexation of CRIMSON by BLUE? This is not discussed.

However, there are suggestions of the fate of Canada in the document. Mentioned three times is that the United States would get Canada in exchange for lost colonial territory, anticipated to be the Philippines, Guam, and Samoa, and perhaps Hawaii and Panama:[331]

From the standpoint of BLUE it would appear to be advantageous for CRIMSON to be allied with RED. In this case BLUE would be free to employ her greatly superior man-power in overrunning CRIMSON and holding that Dominion to offset such losses as BLUE might suffer elsewhere.[332]

The conquest of CRIMSON would probably be held by BLUE more than sufficient to offset probable losses elsewhere.[333]

... the occupation of CRIMSON territory would secure to BLUE a counterbalance against possible territorial losses elsewhere.[334]

There is no mention of annexation in the text. But given the extent and continuity of Manifest Destiny in US history, it seems a likely consideration for the military planners. Certainly, the 1924 military planning document outlining the scope and direction of *War Plan Red* explicitly stated that the "Dominion government will be abolished" and that "the policy will be to prepare the provinces and territories ... to become states and territories of the Blue union."[335]

War Plan Red identifies the characteristics of Canada that make it an easy military acquisition:

---

[331] Ibid., p. 28.
[332] Ibid., p. 7.
[333] Ibid., p. 26.
[334] Ibid., p. 57.
[335] R.A. Preston (1977) *The Defence of the Undefended Border: Planning for War in North America 1867-1939*, Montreal: McGill-Queen's University Press, p. 221.

CRIMSON itself occupies an extremely weak position with respect to BLUE. While its territory is of great extent, all well developed parts thereof lie close to the BLUE border, hence, they are especially vulnerable to attack from BLUE.[336]

The conquest of Canada was not seen to require the military occupation of all of Canada. Rather it was concluded that rapid attack was to be employed to strategically segment the country and to acquire control of critical chokepoints. The east was to be controlled by the capture of Halifax, Montreal and Quebec, and by the isolation of the Atlantic provinces from the rest of Canada:

The great salient into Eastern CRIMSON formed by the state of Maine would provide BLUE with a base from which to conduct operations to cut communications between the Quebec-Montreal area and the Maritime Provinces.[337]

Control of the Montreal-Quebec area would cut off practically all of CRIMSON from RED and would deprive the Maritime Provinces of support and supplies from the rest of CRIMSON.[338]

Ontario was to be controlled by the capture of the Niagara hydro-electric power supply, the Ottawa and St. Lawrence valleys, and the "rail bottle neck" of Winnipeg.[339] The West was to be controlled by the capture of Vancouver. The United States would not dissipate a large force conquering the entire country:

The occupation by BLUE of CRIMSON territory other than the areas enumerated in this subparagraph would not be sufficiently advantageous to offset the disadvantage inherent in the dispersion of effort involved. If initial operations in CRIMSON are successful, BLUE may extend operations to other CRIMSON territory.[340]

The plan identified winter as a major potential problem in the conquest of Canada:

---

[336] *War Plan Red.*, p. 3.
[337] Ibid., p. 3.
[338] Ibid., p. 57.
[339] Ibid., p. 3.
[340] Ibid., p. 57.

On account of the severe winter climate of this portion of CRIMSON, the St. Lawrence River and the Gulf are closed to navigation for several months of each year.[341]

In the important northeastern area the winters are severe, particularly in the northern part. Winter operations on a large scale would be attended with tremendous difficulties in that region.[342]

As already noted, the BLUE northeastern area, which is nearest the most important CRIMSON areas, is, in general well adapted for troop concentrations and movements ... The severe winter climate probably is the most unfavorable factor.[343]

If the outbreak of war occurred in winter, ... operations in CRIMSON territory would be attended with great difficulty.[344]

Clearly, the US military planners conceive winter to be one of the natural defensive assets of Canada.

US motivations for war are discussed and do illustrate the US strategic planning attitude towards Canada. The war plan states that the fundamental reason for the United States to resort to armed conflict is to expand commerce and acquire unfettered access to natural resources. The war plan is quite explicit on the point that aggression must be masked by defensive explanations:

The probable ultimate causes of war between RED and BLUE have been previously estimated to arise out of BLUE competition and interference with RED foreign trade, although other proximate causes to war may be alleged.[345]

Further evidence that the United States considered itself the probable aggressor appears in Section III "Time of Execution":

M-Day is the first day of open mobilization and is the Time Origin for the execution of this JOINT ARMY AND NAVY BASIC WAR PLAN - RED. M-Day may precede a Declaration of War.[346]

War Plan Red details the danger to the United States of a united Commonwealth attack from bases in Canada: "Geographically,

---

[341] Ibid., p. 3.
[342] Ibid., p. 36.
[343] Ibid.
[344] Ibid., p. 60.
[345] Ibid., p. 41.
[346] Ibid., p. 79.

CRIMSON affords RED admirable bases for Naval, Military, and Air Forces close to the vital area of BLUE."[347] However, the plan then declares that it would be a disadvantage for the United States if Canada declared neutrality and did not threaten the United States: "CRIMSON neutrality would be of little military advantage to BLUE."[348] Furthermore, in the event that Canada did not threaten the United States, *War Plan Red* still required that Canada be militarily occupied:

Unless CRIMSON goes so far as to declare her independence of RED and to ally herself with BLUE, it would appear to be advantageous not to accept such neutrality unless accompanied by guarantees. Among such guarantees BLUE should demand and insist upon occupation ... [349]

War Plan Red also identifies those characteristics of the United States which make it warlike:

BLUE's national political organization is well adapted to making war. The BLUE nation is essentially homogeneous, confident, aggressive and resourceful.[350]

Internally, there is little risk of dissent:

The large number of RED citizens residing in the United States and a small number of professional pacifists and communists would be the only elements with which it would be necessary to deal internally.[351]

The foreign policy of the United States, as stated in the document, is particularly threatening to Canada.

It is primarily concerned with the advancement of the foreign trade of BLUE and demands equality of treatment in all political dependencies and backward countries, and unrestricted access to sources of raw materials.[352]

"Unrestricted access" to resources is exactly the same expression used in the current discussions of the need to annex Canada.[353]

---

[347] Ibid., p. 2.
[348] Ibid., p. 7.
[349] Ibid.
[350] Ibid., p. 38.
[351] Ibid.
[352] Ibid., p. 39.
[353] M. Cetron and O. Davies (1989) *American Renaissance: Our Life at the Turn of the 21st Century*, New York: St.Martin's Press, p. 224.

From the document, it appears that the US military planners of the day had a particular interest in the resources of northern Canada. Several times there is focused discussion of the Sudbury nickel mines, which are noted to produce "over ninety percent of the world's supply."[354] Combat operations are specifically directed at Sudbury:

Unless nickel can be obtained from the SUDBURY mines, a serious shortage in that important war-making material will develop in BLUE within a few months after war begins.[355]

It would be particularly advantageous to BLUE to seize at an early date in the war the Sudbury nickel mines in CRIMSON in order to provide a sufficient supply of this most important alloy metal as well as to deny this supply to RED.[356]

Also, there is a surprising mention of "the expected development of the hydro-electric power in the James Bay area."[357] This is in a US war plan developed in the 1920s, four decades before such hydro-electric development was actually begun. It should be noted that it was US business interests, hidden behind corporate fronts, that eventually did initiate the James Bay projects.[358]

Finally, there is an incredible reference to the use of chemical warfare against Canadians. In the original 1930 draft of *War Plan Red*, the use of poison gas was restricted to a second-strike, reactive posture. The US Army was directed, in bold type:

TO MAKE ALL NECESSARY PREPARATIONS FOR THE EFFECTIVE USE OF CHEMICAL WARFARE FROM THE OUTBREAK OF THE WAR BUT TO EMPLOY TOXIC CHEMICAL AGENTS ONLY IF AND WHEN RED ADOPTS THEIR USE.[359]

This was soon to be changed to a first-use directive.

---

[354] *War Plan Red*, p. 10.
[355] Ibid., p. 42.
[356] Ibid., p. 56.
[357] Ibid., p. 3.
[358] R. Davis, M. Zannis, and R. Surette (1974) "Why David Rockefeller was in Quebec City," in R. Chodos and R. Murphy (eds.), *Let Us Prey* (pp. 94-107). Toronto: James Lorimer and Company.
[359] *War Plan Red.*, p. 85.

1935. A VERY BAD YEAR

War Plan Red cannot be dismissed as just an abstract exercise that was made and then put on the shelf or tossed into the wastebasket. This was officially and formally adopted as US military policy. It was updated and amended as needed. There is evidence that concrete preparations were actively pursued. For example, citing a memorandum for the Chief of Staff, Preston reports:

On January 2, 1931, five months before Sutherland-Brown's Defence Scheme Number 1 was withdrawn in Canada, American army officers began to work on a special mobilization plan for invasion of the Dominion.[360]

A revised "War Department Mobilization Plan — 1933" was amended to the section of *War Plan Red* directing the Army to construct and maintain the bases necessary for war on Canada.[361]

In 1934, *War Plan Red* preparations accelerated. In September, officers of the First and Second Armies held a Command Post Exercise (CPX) in New Jersey and "fought an extensive paper war" enacting war plan scenarios.[362] Whether as a result of these exercises or not, a proposal was put to the Joint Board on October 17, 1934, that "we will increase our advantages and hasten the successful ending of the war" if the first-use of nerve gas is authorized.[363] On November 7, 1934, the Joint Board approved amending *War Plan Red* to allow the Army, in bold type, the first-use of nerve gas, at the earliest possible time:

TO MAKE ALL NECESSARY PREPARATIONS FOR THE USE OF CHEMICAL WARFARE FROM THE OUTBREAK OF THE WAR. THE USE OF CHEMICAL WARFARE, INCLUDING THE USE OF TOXIC AGENTS, FROM THE INCEPTION OF HOSTILITIES, IS AUTHORIZED, SUBJECT TO SUCH RESTRICTIONS OR PROHIBITIONS AS MAY BE CONTAINED IN ANY DULY RATIFIED

---

[360] R.A. Preston (1977) *The Defence of the Undefended Border: Planning for War in North America 1867-1939*, Montreal: McGill-Queen's University Press, pp. 224-225.
[361] *War Plan Red*, p. 89, amended.
[362] Anon. (1935) "Army Navy Plan Huge War Games," *New York Times*, April 15, p. 4.
[363] Commander A.S. Carpender and Colonel W. Krueger (1934) [untitled memo to the Joint Board appended to *War Plan Red*], Oct. 17, p. 1.

INTERNATIONAL CONVENTION OR CONVENTIONS WHICH AT THE TIME MAY BE BINDING UPON THE UNITED STATES AND THE ENEMY STATE OR STATES.[364]

Considering that such conventions were never ratified, that the US Army's theatre of operations was in Canada, and that US plans for the onset of war presumed that Canadian allies would not yet have arrived in force, this amendment is an explicit authorization for the use of gas warfare against Canadians. This was deliberated, planned and approved during a time of peace and goodwill between Canada and the United States, a time when "peace bridges" were being built across the Niagara and St. Lawrence rivers. Clearly, there is little ground upon which to base faith that US military planning has been, is, or would be beneficent towards Canadians. Expedience is the order of the day.

Two months later, on January 18, 1935, the US War Department announced that it was going to double the size of Pine Camp by the purchase of up to 10,000 acres.[365] On February 20, 1935, it is announced that Pine Camp will be the site for summer maneuvres for 60,000 men, the entire First Army.[366] This would be by far the largest peacetime military maneuvres in US history. One month later the press is told that the maneuvres are being held at Pine Camp only because there is not enough room in New Jersey.[367] In fact, the actual maneuvres at Pine Camp would only involve about half the numbers of men first estimated. Thus, in circular logic, the expansion of Pine Camp justified its selection for maneuvres, which was justified by its expansion, all to accommodate highly inflated estimates of participating manpower. It would seem that base expansion was a military priority and maneuvres were the means.

[364] War Plan Red, p. 85 amended.
[365] Anon. (1935) "May Enlarge Pine Camp," New York Times, January 19, p. 15.
[366] Anon. (1935) "Plans Army Maneuvre: War Department Picks Pine Camp N.Y., for Drill of 60,000 Men," New York Times, February 20, p. 2.
[367] Anon. (1935) "Army to Mass 60,000 in Record War Game: Mammoth Maneuvres Planned for Northern New York, with Nolan in Charge," New York Times, March 20, p. 22.

Coincident with these developments, the US Army was pushing a bill through Congress to create new air bases. According to Preston, the Army Air Force had been doubtful of *War Plan Red* because it did not give adequate consideration to the fact that US mobilization of the aircraft industry would be much slower than British mobilization and movement of aircraft reinforcements to Canada.[368] The solution to this problem was to build a forward air force base on the Canadian border in the Great Lakes region for offensive preemptive strikes against Canadian airfields. It was to be "camouflaged" as a civilian airport used by military aircraft for refueling during transcontinental flights.

On February 11 to 13, the Committee on Military Affairs of the House of Representatives heard secret testimony from high ranking military officers on a bill to build new air bases at a cost of $19,000,000 each. At the time of the hearings, the press was told that Brigadier General Charles Kilbourne, retiring head of the War Plans Division, had requested only six new bases and had argued for a change of wording that "gave the Secretary of War authority, within limits, to establish air bases where he saw fit."[369] This discretionary power was not incidental. It was to allow an unreported seventh base to be built on the Canadian border for preemptive attacks on Canadian targets. The revised bill passed in the House of Representatives on March 28.[370]

Although the general's testimony was supposed to have been secret, the verbatim transcript was published by the government printing office.[371] Apparently, due to the absence of the committee

[368] R.A. Preston (1977) *The Defence of the Undefended Border: Planning for War in North America 1867-1939*, Montreal: McGill-Queen's University Press, p. 224.
[369] Anon. (1935) "Army Proposes 6 New Air Bases: Brigadier General Speaking to House Military Affairs Committee," *New York Times*, Feb. 12, p. 5.
[370] Anon. (1935) "Bigger Navy Bills Passed by House," *New York Times*, March 28, p. 1.
[371] Anon. (1935) *Hearings before the Committee on Military Affairs House of Representatives, Seventy-Fourth Congress, First Session, on H.R. 6621 and H.R. 4230, February 11, 12, 13, 1935*. Washington, DC: United States Government Printing Office.

chairman, to clerical error, to committee member connivance, or to some combination of these, the closed sessions were not deleted from the public copy.[372] This secret testimony by General Kilbourne and several other military officers is another window into US military designs on Canada.

The Army wanted six air bases identified by region: (1) Atlantic Northeast, (2) Caribbean-Panama, (3) Southeast, (4) Pacific Northwest, (5) Alaska and (6) Rocky Mountains. The seventh base was identified in the bill as "(7) such intermediate stations as will in connection with (6), provide for transcontinental movements incident to the concentration of the General Headquarters Air Force for maneuvres."[373] In reviewing the history of the bill, Kilbourne noted that Major General Hugh Drum, for whom Fort Drum was eventually named, chaired the 1933 board that directed the Air Corps to establish strategic air bases appropriate for existing war plan scenarios.[374] After the committee chairman made a strong statement "that Congress would be emphatic in insisting that defense, and defense only, is the attitude with regard to any feature of national defense,"[375] General Kilbourne carefully explained the duplicity required in putting air bases on the Canadian border:

I have indicated before that we want to establish a base in the northeast area and one in the northwest. We would like to put one close to the Great Lakes, but we must avoid going too far in establishing new military stations close to the northern border, and limit ourselves to those essential in peace-time training operations. So we would have one in New England, on the New England coast, and in the West to actually contact with Alaska, but when it comes to the intermediate stations we put them down to enable the air force to go from coast to coast.

---

[372] Anon. (1935) "Roosevelt Scores House Committee on Border Air Base," *New York Times*, May 1, pp. 1, 8.
   Anon. (1935) "M'Swain Explains Canada Incident,"*New York Times*, May 2, p. 11.
[373] Anon. (1935) *Hearings before the Committee on Military Affairs House of Representatives, Seventy-Fourth Congress, First Session, on H.R. 6621 and H.R. 4230, February 11, 12, 13, 1935.* Washington, DC: United States Government Printing Office, p. 12.
[374] Ibid., p. 13.
[375] Ibid., p. 15.

We do not want to accentuate anything that would look as though we contemplated passing away from the century-old principle that our Canadian border needs no defense.

The War Department is very much interested in the development of those two, and we do hope that a lot of our air-defense planning will be done in the extension of our commercial facilities and private flying fields....

We cannot go out in the military line along the Canadian border, but we can legitimately extend the advantages of landing fields and commercial fields to the people who are on the border. I think we could do that without attracting any attention.

I am explaining why the proposed substitute is worded the way it is, accentuating in every way training in peace time....[376]

When Congressman Wilcox said to the general, "Your bill is more flexible than mine as to the number of planes and personnel that would be used at various places,"[377] Kilbourne replied:

I would have been very glad to put in the bill the Great Lakes area, but I could not put it in the bill because of the Canadian situation. You will notice no. 7 in my bill is camouflaged. It is called "intermediate" stations for transcontinental flights, but it means the same thing.[378]

In a later closed session, the committee heard testimony from Captain Harold Lee George, from the Air Corps Practice School. He gave an extensive recitation of *War Plan Red* presumptions that a British alliance might launch bomber attacks on the United States from sites in Canada, Labrador, Bermuda, the Bahamas and the Lesser Antilles. The only defence, he argued, is the creation of an air force that is capable of preemptive surprise attacks on enemy launch sites.[379] General F.M. Andrews, commander of the Army Air Force, continued explaining the *War Plan Red* scenario, throwing France into the alliance against the United States. Nazi Germany never appears to have entered into US military contingency planning:

---

[376] Ibid., pp. 16-17.
[377] Ibid., p. 22.
[378] Ibid.
[379] Ibid., p. 55.

115

With Canada involved on the side of the hostile coalition, many land bases and sheltered water bases are available. But, even with Canada neutral, the enemy has the following bases available: Newfoundland.... St.Pierre and Miquelon.... Bermuda.... Bahamas Islands.... Jamaica.... Trinidad... British Honduras... The Lesser Antilles, British and French.... [380]

He downplayed hostile intentions towards Canada, but argued:

... air force operations from a base in the Great Lakes area would be capable of dominating the industrial heart of Canada, the Ontario Peninsula, and prevent the establishment of enemy air bases in that area.... [381]

Colonel Walter Krueger, Assistant Chief of Staff in Charge of the War Plans Division, was the last to give testimony. This is the same Colonel Krueger who recommended to the Joint Board four months earlier that the authorized early use of nerve gas would hasten the successful conquest of Canada. In his testimony, he tried to pacify Congressmen concerned about the offensiveness of the proposed expansion of bases along the Canadian border:

Our G.H.Q. [General Head Quarters] air force cannot by any stretch of the imagination be considered a weapon of conquest, considering its own inherent limitation. It is bound by these limitations, such, for instance, as that an air force could not go somewhere and light on the ground and occupy that territory. It just cannot be done.

But considering its limitation in that connection, together with our geographical position, our G.H.Q. air force is, par excellence, a defensive weapon. That it operates tactically on the offensive is clear to anyone.

But I do not believe that any man who knows anything about it visualizes a situation where we are going to project the G.H.Q. air force into some other country to seize and hold territory in that country. [382]

As documents appended to *War Plan Red* show, Colonel Krueger was clearly and intentionally deceiving Congress with this testimony. On March 6, 1935, General Douglas MacArthur, Chief of Staff, recommended tactical changes to *War Plan Red*,[383] which Colonel Krueger approved on April 10 on behalf of the Joint

---

[380] Ibid., p. 60.
[381] Ibid., p. 61.
[382] Ibid., p. 88.
[383] General D. MacArthur (1935) [untitled memo to the Joint Board appended to *War Plan Red*], March 6.

Planning Committee.[384] The changes, approved by the US Secretary of War and Secretary of the Navy on May 9,[385] specified the following about any decision to execute *War Plan Red:*

The carrying out of the decision will include: a) By the *Army* - A maximum Army concentration in the Northeast section of the UNITED STATES, with forces so disposed as to facilitate:

(1) An early joint overseas expedition against Halifax in case the situation at the outbreak of war justifies such an operation. If not, then an operation to secure the Moncton Area, with Halifax as the ultimate objective.

(2) An early operation to secure the Montreal-Quebec area.

(3) Immediate air operations on as large a scale as practicable, in support of one or both of the operations contemplated in sub-paragraphs (1) and (2) above, or in lieu of that contemplated in sub-paragraph (1).[386]

Air operations were thought to substitute for land occupation. In other words, the US military did plan to "project" their newly expanded air force into "some other country" to help "seize and hold territory in that country."

Allocation specifications provided by Colonel Krueger showed that the Great Lakes base would have five hangars and housing for 85 officers, 119 noncommissioned officers and 600 enlisted men.[387] That would have been a moderate sized air base in its day. It has yet to be identified where in the Great Lakes region this base was to have been built, or where it was actually built.

The House Military Affairs Committee's hearings became public in April 1935 and made international news.[388] Dramatically highlighting the contrast between public words of friendship vs. secret planning for war, the US Under Secretary of State gave a prepared speech the

---

[384] Colonel W. Krueger and Captain J. Smeallie (1935) [untitled memo to the Joint Board], April 10.

[385] J. Butler (1935) [untitled letter to the Secretary of War appended to *War Plan Red*], May 10.

[386] *War Plan Red*, as amended, p. 82.

[387] Anon. (1935) *Hearings before the Committee on Military Affairs House of Representatives, Seventy-Fourth Congress, First Session, on H.R. 6621 and H.R. 4230, February 11, 12, 13, 1935*. Washington, DC: United States Government Printing Office, p. 95.

[388] Anon, (1935) "Air Base Provided Near Canada Line:'Camouflage' Clause is Disclosed as Put into Wilcox Bill by War Department," *New York Times*, April 29, p. 2.

next day praising the Rush-Bagot Agreement of 1817 for successfully limiting military forces in the Lake Champlain and Great Lakes regions.[389] Through deliberate ignorance or deliberate deceit, President Roosevelt claimed that the US had no military plans directed against Canada and that those generals were just giving personal opinions.[390] His letter to the House Military Affairs Committee was published in the *New York Times*:

This government does not in any of its plans or policies envisage the possibility of a change in the friendly relationship between the United States and any foreign country.

I call your especial attention to the fact that this government not only accepts as an accomplished fact the permanent peace conditions cemented by many generations of friendship between the Canadian and American people, but expects to live up to not only the letter but the spirit of our treaties relating to the permanent disarmament of our three thousand miles of common boundary.[391]

However, Roosevelt forcefully defended secret military planning and threatened Congress that military staff would be forbidden to testify to Congress if secret testimony could not be kept secret.[392] Publication of Roosevelt's letter to the committee in the *New York Times* was deemed by the US State Department to be "ample notification to Canada of the government's position."[393]

The Canadian response was disbelief and later laughter. Hume Wrong, Council of the Canadian Legation, asked the US State Department for the transcripts of the testimony, but emphasized to the press "that he had asked for no documents or data considered secret or confidential."[394] Even though the controversial testimony explicitly emphasized the importance of the location of air bases on

---

[389] Anon. (1935) "Canadian Treaty Held World Ideal," *New York Times*, April 30, p. 10.
[390] Anon. (1935) "Roosevelt Scores House Committee on Border Air Base," *New York Times*, May 1, pp. 1, 8.
[391] Ibid., p. 8.
[392] Ibid.
[393] Ibid.
[394] Anon. (1935) "Canada Asks Data on Air Base Proposal," *New York Times*, April 30, p. 10.

the Canadian border, a Canadian flying ace told the *New York Times*:

Location of air bases doesn't mean a thing. With long range machines, the United States could have her bases on the Gulf of Mexico and still reach Canada without difficulty.[395]

This is remarkably like some current comments about the Fort Drum expansion.

The first official word to be reported from Ottawa was:

The government.... had been disposed from the first not to take the matter seriously except for its possible effect on Canadian public opinion.[396]

Sir George Parley, acting Prime Minister, was quoted as saying:

No one in Canada believed the Government of the United States had any intentions of departing from the attitude which has been officially termed "the policy of good neighbors."[397]

This see-no-evil, hear-no-evil attitude was reflected in the Canadian press. For example, the *Globe and Mail* headlined the story "US Disavows Airport Yarn," even when it was confirmed to them that the bill would be passed and the air bases constructed.[398] The *Toronto Globe* wrote that it was all just "foolish publicity given to an irritating subject," and the *Montreal Gazette* wrote:

Canadians by and large did not take the episode seriously and were inclined rather to laugh heartily at the absurdity of the whole affair.[399]

The various US explanations for the border base testimony were lame, contradictory, and in the retrospective light of *War Plan Red*, simply false. First, President Roosevelt denied that the United States had military plans against Canada or any intentions to build a forward air base on the border[400] even though *War Plan Red* was

[395] Ibid.
[396] Anon. (1935) "Action Pleases Canada: Roosevelt Stand is Held to Meet Public Opinion," *New York Times,*" May 1, p. 8.
[397] Anon. (1935) "M'Swain Explains Canada Incident," *New York Times,* May 2, p. 11.
[398] Anon. (1935) "US Disavows Airport Yarn," *Globe and Mail,* May 1, p. 1.
[399] J. MacCormac (1935) "Canadians Amused by Air Base Talk," *New York Times,* May 5, sec. IV, p. 7.
[400] Anon. (1935) "Roosevelt Scores House Committee on Border Air Base," *New York Times,* May 1, pp. 1, 8.

official military policy and the proposed base was explicitly hostile to Canada. Then the two generals, one in charge of US War Plans and the other in charge of the Air Force, "declared that they were expressing only their personal views."[401] General Andrews said that his testimony was "abstract military study with no concrete political thought or reference."[402] The committee chairman explained that the base was like the French fortifications on the Belgian border, "not against Belgium but against what might come over or through Belgium."[403] In fact, the French had not extended Maginot Line fortifications along the Belgian border.[404] And the Maginot Line, a massive system of trenches and bunkers, is clearly defensive; whereas a forward, secret air force base is clearly offensive.

The border air base issue did not end there. One month later, the United States was considering a site for a new air base in the Lake Champlain region south of Montreal, where Plattsburgh Air Force Base is now located.[405] The Canadian government's response to this report, when questioned in the Canadian Senate, was that US air bases are their own domestic matter.[406] One month later, President Roosevelt showed his satisfaction with General Kilbourne's performance by recommending him for promotion.[407]

Still more happened in 1935. Because of the emphasis in *War Plan Red* on speed and surprise, the US Department of War identified rapid mobilization to be critically important. Mobilization planning was initiated in 1931 and a new mobilization plan was amended to *War Plan Red* in 1933. In June 1935, the US Army was expanded

---

[401] Ibid., p. 8.
[402] Ibid.
[403] Anon, (1935) "M'Swain Explains Canada Incident," New York Times, May 2, p. 11.
[404] R.A. Preston (1977) The Defence of the Undefended Border: Planning for War in North America 1867-1939, Montreal: McGill-Queen's University Press, p. 225.
[405] Anon. (1935) "Studies Big Air Base in Lake Champlain," New York Times, June 9, p. 21.
[406] Anon. (1935) "Canada Unruffled by Air Base," New York Times, June 13, p. 13.
[407] Anon. (1935) "Gets Army Promotion," New York Times, July 24, p. 3.

by adding another 299 soldiers to each military post, including Madison Barracks, Fort Ontario, and Plattsburgh Barracks, bringing the total force to 165,000.[408] Later in 1935 and 1936, the Army War College prepared a "critical" atlas of Canada, showing invasion routes and the disposition of Canadian military units and their strengths.[409]

Also in 1935, the largest peacetime military maneuvers in US history were announced. The site? Fort Drum, as it is now known.[410] More than 36,000 militia and regular army troops — five divisions — converged on northern New York using trains, convoys, and even a fleet of 269 New York City taxis that raced across New York State to pick up troops in Buffalo to rush them to the northern border.[411] The scale of these maneuvers was immense. Simultaneously with this mobilization, another 15,000 troops were called to maneuvres in Pennsylvania "to act as strategic reserve for the larger force" on the Canadian border.[412] It should be noted that *War Plan Red*, as amended, called for "a concentration in the New York-New England area" for "offensive operations on a large scale" against Montreal[413] and for the "concentration of approximately one Army corps as a general reserve."[414]

Most people now, of course, would presume that this mobilization exercise was in preparation for war in Europe. But mobilization for shipment to an overseas war would not take such a form, certainly not taxi cabs racing around to get reservists to the front. More importantly, at that time, the United States, both in official policy and in popular opinion, was isolationist and determined not to get

[408] Anon. (1935) "299 Men to be Added at Post," *Watertown Daily Times*, June 29, p. 6.
[409] R.A. Preston (1977) *The Defence of the Undefended Border: Planning for War in North America 1867-1939*, Montreal: McGill-Queen's University Press, p. 225.
[410] Anon. (1935) "Capitol Regards Maneuvers Well," *Watertown Daily Times*, August 27, p. 22
[411] H.W. Baldwin (1935) "Troops Mobilize for Big War Games," *New York Times*, August 18, pp. 1-2.
[412] Ibid.
[413] *War Plan Red*, as amended, p. 86.
[414] Ibid., p. 87.

involved in another European war. Wrote Preston: "Hence there was little or no work on Army Plan Black for war with Germany."[415]

At the time of the 1935 maneuvres, it was common knowledge, widely used in the newspapers, that the opposing armies had been coded Blue and Red. It was not known or reported that Blue indicated US forces and Red indicated forces in Canada defending Canada. Not reported in the press, but published in the souvenir pamphlet for the maneuvres, was the *War Plan Red* scenario of Blue US forces invading Canada and confronting Red defensive forces:

Major General Nolan, who outlined the situation confronting each force, assumed a blue foreign army advancing across a feigned international boundary defended by a red army.[416]

The "war" opened with a Blue motorized assault across the international border.[417] Red forces initially drove the invading Blue forces back.[418] As with the 1908 maneuvres, the war games were scripted for Blue reinforcements to arrive and the Red forces to lose "outnumbered and out-gunned."[419] Thus goes the theoretical and practiced conquest of Canada. As with the 1908 and 1910 maneuvres, the weather disrupted the 1935 maneuvres when "torrential rains washed out the war games."[420] But foul weather has never disrupted military plans for Fort Drum, and the War Department purchased another 9,000 acres of land.[421]

---

[415] R.A. Preston (1977) *The Defence of the Undefended Border: Planning for War in North America 1867-1939*, Montreal: McGill-Queen's University Press, p. 219.

[416] Anon. (1935) *Souvenir of the First Army Maneuvers: The Greatest Peace Time Event in US Military History at Pine Camp, N.Y., August, 1935*, Watertown, N.Y.: Santway Photo-Craft Co., p. 2.

[417] H.W. Baldwin (1935) "Motorized Attack Opens Modern 'War'," *New York Times*, August 22, pp. 1,3.

[418] J.H. Brior (1935) "Reds Drive Back New Englanders," *Watertown Daily Times*, August 22, p. 1.

[419] Anon. (1935) *Souvenir of the First Army Maneuvers: The Greatest Peace Time Event in US Military History at Pine Camp, N.Y., August, 1935*, Watertown, N.Y.: Santway Photo-Craft Co., p. 2.

[420] J.H. Brior (1935) "War Games End in Sea of Mud," *Watertown Daily Times*, August 27, p. 1.

[421] Anon. (1988) *10th Mountain Division (L.I.) and Fort Drum: An Unofficial Directory and Guide Published for Fort Drum Newcomers*, South Boston, VI: B. Hunt Enterprises.

In 1936, agreement was reached between Canada and the United States on initial steps towards free trade.[422] In 1937, the Army added a second airfield to Pine Camp.[423] That same year, the Thousand Islands Peace Bridge was begun. Also in 1937, *War Plan Red* was withdrawn in favor of a new plan against Canada which conceived that France would join England in defence of Canada as suggested in the 1935 testimony to Congress.[424] The new plan emphasized the objective of seizing control of the St. Lawrence River. In 1938, the Thousand Islands Peace Bridge was completed, and President Roosevelt at the dedication made new promises of peace and goodwill.[425] In 1939, as Canada was going to war against Nazi aggression in Europe, the US Army and Naval War Colleges perfected operational plans for a US expeditionary force to capture Halifax.[426]

LESSONS

This five decades of documented military planning and preparation against a smaller, peaceful neighbour nation is shocking and shameful. It is not something to be proud of, and certainly not something to be easily excused or explained. US war plans against Canada were treachery of the first order. The US citizenry are ever angry about the Japanese attack on Pearl Harbor, but at least the United States knew Japan was a belligerent nation on unfriendly terms. The US military had been expecting war with Japan for almost four decades before it happened. Hearings before the House

[422] E. Kierans and W. Stewart (1988) *Wrong End of the Rainbow: The Collapse of Free Enterprise in Canada*, Toronto: Collins.

[423] Anon. (1937) "Government Buys Flying Field," *New York Times*, April 17, p. 6.

[424] R.A. Preston (1977) *The Defence of the Undefended Border: Planning for War in North America 1867-1939*, Montreal: McGill-Queen's University Press, p. 225.

[425] F.A. Storm (1938) "Roosevelt Pledges that US Will 'Not Stand Idly by' if Canada is Threatened by any Foreign Power," *Watertown Daily Times*, August 18, pp. 1, 20.

[426] R.A. Preston (1977) *The Defence of the Undefended Border: Planning for War in North America 1867-1939*, Montreal: McGill-Queen's University Press, p. 226.

Military Affairs Committee in 1935 even presumed and predicted that the Japanese war would begin with a carrier-based surprise attack on US Pacific bases.[427] There was no surprise. But Canada was, is, a nonbellicose nation thinking itself on good terms with the United States, a fact clearly known by US political leadership and US military intelligence.

There is some evidence that elements in the US military in this period had fascist, pro-German leanings that were further encouraged by rightwing organizations such as the American Liberty League which were in turn backed by such corporate interests as the Morgans, du Ponts, Mellons and Rockefellers.[428] In 1934, the United States' most decorated and popular general, Smedly Butler, was approached in his retirement to organize 500,000 US veterans into an American version of the German Brown Shirts, the Italian Black Shirts and the French Crois de Feu. The ultimate objective was to stop President Roosevelt's populist economic reforms, to depose him if necessary. However, Butler revealed all of this to a Congressional committee.[429] Corroborating evidence was found in bank records and internal reports.[430] Butler was ridiculed in the mainstream press, his full testimony was kept from public record, and the plotters were protected from prosecution. The committee chairman, John McCormack, eventually to become Speaker of the House, said in 1971:

There was no doubt that General Butler was telling the truth. We believed his testimony one hundred percent. He was a great, patriotic American in every respect.[431]

---

[427] Anon. (1935) *Hearings before the Committee on Military Affairs House of Representatives, Seventy-Fourth Congress, First Session, on H.R. 6621 and H.R. 4230, February 11, 12, 13, 1935.* Washington, DC: United States Government Printing Office.
[428] J. Archer (1973) *The Plot to Seize the White House*, New York: Hawthorn Books.
[429] Anon. (1935) "Asks Laws to Curb Foreign Agitators," *New York Times.* Feb. 16, pp. 1,4.
[430] J. Archer (1973) *The Plot to Seize the White House*, New York: Hawthorn Books.
[431] Ibid., p. 213.

This episode was the factual basis for the novel, *Seven Days in May*.[432]

One official US military history has tried to claim that war plans against Canada were "abstract exercises," "simply outlines of missions," "meaningless."[433] Such an interpretation overlooks the intelligence gathering, the border violations, the base construction, the maneuvres and the whole mindset of planning the death of Canadians while speaking words of peace and friendship. Such an interpretation overlooks the calculated deception of US citizens and their political representatives. Preston tried to find some silver lining in this dark cloud and argued that some parts of the war plans against Canada were adaptable for war against Germany.[434] He also argued that war planning kept active during peacetime the strategic skills that proved necessary for the prosecution of World War II. But this excuses the very incompetence of US strategic planning, to have such an automatic and obsessive fixation on war with Canada while not noticing the rise of Nazi militarism in Europe.

This history of US duplicity toward Canada has implications for present concerns about Fort Drum. First of all, the very origins of Fort Drum rest on preparations for the conquest of Canada. Fort Drum has a history of hostility. A presumption of continued hostility from Fort Drum is prudent. The US military has long identified this region as the best place from which to attack Canada. The burden of proof is on the United States to show that the base is peaceful.

The second lesson from this history makes such a proof difficult or impossible. This is the lesson of dishonesty and deceit. Neither the US military nor US politicians can be trusted to be truthful. US

---

[432] F. Knebel (1962) *Seven Days in May*, New York: Harper and Row.
[433] R.S. Cline (1951) *Washington Command Post*, Washington, DC: Office of the Chief of Military History, Dept. of the Army, p. 35.
[434] R.A. Preston (1977) *The Defence of the Undefended Border: Planning for War in North America 1867-1939*, Montreal: McGill-Queen's University Press, p. 226.

Presidents Taft, Harding and Roosevelt each explicitly denied US designs against Canada even while their military commanders were actively preparing invasion plans. Either they lied knowingly, or they lied knowing that they choose to be ignorant. Assurances are worth nothing.

A third lesson is that US military preparations against Canada appear to arise from no other consideration than that Canada is a foreign country. The border itself seems to order the US military mind to prepare for war. There is no need to seek rationale for hostile US preparations against Canada. The United States has prepared for war against Canada even in periods of extended peace, when there were no disputes or reasons for war.

That is the fourth lesson. Periods of peace seem to be most dangerous for Canada. When Fort Drum was first created, when it was first expanded, and now during this most recent expansion, peaceful commerce and free trade were the issues of the day. When the US military mind focuses on overseas missions, Canada is relatively safe. When that focus relaxes, the preoccupation with Canada returns.

There are plausible connections between these early war preparations and the recent developments at Fort Drum. When *War Plan Red* was reported by the Syracuse *Post-Standard*, it was suggested that there was a close link:

Just think how much easier it would be if an attack on Canada could start with a fast-moving force heading to Ottawa from a US military base just south of the border.[435]

Although the geopolitical contexts of 1930s and 1980s are very different in many ways, they are similar in others. Both periods are marked by decades of goodwill between Canada and the United States, mutually beneficial commerce, peacefulness and trust. The International Peace Bridge between Buffalo and Fort Erie was

---

[435] J.D. Salant (1991) "The War that Never Was," *The Post-Standard* (Syracuse), March 25, p. A1.

completed in 1926, a new bridge crossing the St. Lawrence River at Cornwall was completed in 1934,[436] and the Thousand Islands Peace Bridge was completed in 1938. Both periods are also marked by US economic failure — the Great Depression in the 1930s and a more chronic loss of competitiveness by the United States in the 1980s. In step with this, both periods are marked by the United States having to face global economic competition — the United Kingdom and Commonwealth in the 1930s, East Asia and a united Europe in the 1980s. A major difference between the periods is that the US population was generally isolationist and antiwar in the 1930s, whereas it is more aggressive and militaristic today. In sum, if the United States could make military preparations to attack Canada in the 1930s, there is little reason to doubt that it could make such preparations in the 1980s.

Elements of *War Plan Red* are coherent with the presumption that Fort Drum forces are directed at military interventions in Canada. Because of the size of Canada, *War Plan Red* emphasized rapid attack on strategic cities. Fort Drum forces are rapid attack forces specializing in urban warfare. *War Plan Red* identified the difficulty of winter operations in Canada. Fort Drum forces are winter equipped and winter trained. At the time of the inception of *War Plan Red*, Fort Drum, then known as Pine Camp, was more a training field than a military base, and there was no convenient bridge across the St. Lawrence River. Thus, there is no mention in *War Plan Red* of a US force from the Watertown region crossing the Thousand Islands. The nearest point of attack into Canada was from the St. Lawrence shore opposite Cornwall, Ontario, approximately 100 kilometers (62 miles) from Fort Drum.[437]

There has been some speculation that the "Peace Bridge" across the Thousand Islands was modified during construction in order to better serve military purposes. One longtime resident of the region,

---

[436] Anon. (1934) "Plans for Bridge Opening Talked," *Watertown Daily Times*, May 2, p. 3.
[437] *War Plan Red*, p. 4.

now in his eighties, claims that during construction of the bridge the stone base for the entrance ramps was increased from the plan specifications of 22 centimeters (9 inches) to 56 centimeters (22 inches) and that people in the construction crews at the time surmised that this was to allow the bridge to be used for military vehicles.[438] The *Toronto Star* tried to check this and did report approximate confirmation of the first figure.[439] Plausible as it may seem that the Thousand Islands Bridge was modified for military purposes, that is unlikely considering that the bridge construction was a local initiative directed by a public corporation without one cent of US federal money.[440] On the other hand, if the US military would build a border air base "camouflaged" as a civilian airport in 1935,[441] they might also have arranged to build a cross-border bridge as a civilian project.

The long US history of peacetime preparations for war against Canada — particularly *War Plan Red*, secret base construction and large scale maneuvres in the 1930s — should end the easy and confident dismissal of concern about Fort Drum. The possibility that the United States would attack Canada has been unbelievable to Canadians and Americans alike because they both know themselves to be good people, democratic, with a tradition of alliance and peace. The Americans just would not ever plan to attack Canada. Who can imagine it? Certainly, the US population is not hostile. Nor are most US politicians. Perhaps even officers and soldiers in the US armed forces would be resistant to an attack on Canada. But military planning is not a public process. It is difficult to know how decisions are made, by whom, and to what ends. The preparation of assault troops at Fort Drum has enough

---

[438] Personal communication, October 4, 1991.

[439] J. Picton (1991) "Is US Base Potential Threat to Canada?" *Toronto Star*, Dec. 1, p. A7.

[440] Thousand Island Bridge Authority (1991), personal communication, Nov. 13.

[441] Anon. (1935) *Hearings before the Committee on Military Affairs House of Representatives, Seventy-Fourth Congress, First Session, on H.R. 6621 and H.R. 4230, February 11, 12, 13, 1935*. Washington, DC: United States Government Printing Office.

inconsistencies and irregularities that it deserves careful scrutiny by people of goodwill on both sides of the border. No one can say that US military planners would never consider attacking Canada. They have. For decades. At times more unlikely than our own.

CHAPTER 9

US INTRIGUE AND THREAT

From a US perspective, there are two scenarios that could easily justify military intervention in Canada. One is the secession of Quebec and any accompanying civil disorder. The other is endangered access to vital Canadian resources, particularly energy and water. There is evidence that the US has, during the past few decades, actually prepared or threatened military intervention in Canada for these very concerns.

TASK FORCE REVOLT

In the early 1960s, the Kennedy administration re-oriented US military and security services towards "counterinsurgency." Well-known products of this policy were the Green Berets and the Peace Corps. Less well-known were research programs to understand, predict and control social revolution, political upheaval and internal war. In 1964, the Special Operations Research Office (SORO) of the US Department of Defense undertook a widescale, international study of societies in the process of change and revolution. Project Camelot, as it was code named, had a $6,000,000 budget just for its feasibility study, making it the "largest single set of grants ever directed to a social science study."[442] The project collapsed within one year when some social scientists revealed its intent and scope to foreign politicians and media. Concern about the ethics of military research and research funding reverberated for several years.[443]

Quebec was one of the target societies of study, along with a host of Latin American countries, including Cuba, Chile, Bolivia and Colombia.[444] Cuba and Quebec were selected as the two test cases for the feasibility study. The Quebec plan was called "Task Force Revolt." It eventually became publicly known that the US Army was studying Quebec separatism and the project was killed. There is speculation that the plan was leaked by the State Department in order to frustrate its rivals in the Department of Defense.[445]

Jean-François Lisée, in his book *In the Eye of the Eagle*, concluded that the US Army was never really interested in Quebec.[446] Rather, he argues that "Task Force Revolt" was the result of the enthusiasm of one lone Franco-American, Normand Lacharité, given too much rein by the US Department of Defense. However, when Ottawa was calling out the troops in October 1970, Bolivia experienced a military coup that same month. And again in 1971. In 1973, the US military engineered a coup against the democratically elected Allende government in Chile. The fact that US military planners put Quebec in the same category with Chile,

---

[442] S. Bok (1984) *Secrets: On the Ethics of Concealment and Revelation*, Oxford: Oxford University Press, p. 236.

[443] I.L. Horowitz (1967) *The Rise and Fall of Project Camelot: Studies in the Relationship between Social Sciences and Practical Politics*, Cambridge, Mass.: M.I.T. Press.

R.L. Beale (1969) *Politics of Social Research: An Inquiry into the Ethics and Responsibilities of Social Scientists*, Chicago: Aldine Pub.

[444] B. Macadam and J.R. Dubro (1974) "How the CIA has us Spooked," *Maclean's*, July, pp. 20, 42-44, 46.

J.-F. Lisée (1990) *In the Eye of the Eagle*, Toronto: Harper Collins.

[445] B. Macadam and J.R. Dubro (1974) "How the CIA has us Spooked," *Maclean's*, July, pp. 20, 42-44, 46.

[446] J.-F. Lisée (1990) *In the Eye of the Eagle*, Toronto: Harper Collins.

Bolivia and Cuba has ominous implications for an independent Quebec.

CRISIS IN QUEBEC

There have been numerous retrospective accounts of the crisis of October 1970, when FLQ[447] kidnappings and murder ostensibly justified Prime Minister Trudeau in declaring martial law. However, there are still unanswered questions about the US role in that. The October Crisis was a bizarre episode in Canadian history that has never been fully explained. Six days after the War Measures Act was invoked, Justice Minister John Turner said, "It might not ever be possible to disclose to the public the information on which the government made its decision."[448]

Although the questions and the existing leads are provocative, they have received little followup. For example, in 1973, the *Toronto Star*'s award-winning reporter Tom Hazlitt published an exclusive interview with Jim Bennett, the director of the RCMP's anti-espionage operations during the October Crisis. Bennett reportedly claimed:

That during the separatist crisis of October, 1970, in Montreal, the Canadian security services had to assign much-needed investigators to the task of shadowing agents of the US Central Intelligence Agency, who had infiltrated Montreal on a large scale and were carrying on operations without the approval of the Canadian government.

That during the same crisis the Canadian government moved tanks and other heavy equipment into position south of Ottawa to offset a build-up of American tanks and heavy equipment just south of the US border.[449]

The *Star* report added the comment:

---

[447] "Front de la Liberation du Québec" or "FLQ" refers to a radical terrorist organization committed to the secession of Quebec from Canada.

[448] J. Littleton (1986) *Target Nation: Canada and the Western Intelligence Network*, Toronto: Lester and Orpen Dennys, p. 130.

[449] T. Hazlitt (1973) "Ex-Spy Claims US Tanks Ready in Quebec Crisis," *Toronto Star*, Sept. 22, pp. A1, A4.

Canadian newspaper accounts at the time of the crisis abound in references to the movement of heavy equipment in and around Ottawa, including some movements which military spokesmen insisted were routine exercises. An armed forces spokesman in Ottawa said that while the military presence at the time was well-documented, it was not in the public interest to describe specific movements, strengths or equipment.[450]

The report also carried a brief front page companion piece containing denials by Ottawa and a lightly veiled threat by a very senior, but unnamed, government official against Bennett for discussing any of the events surrounding the October Crisis:

I seriously question the propriety of Bennett discussing intelligence matters at all. He is bound by the Official Secrets Act, which extends to the grave and perhaps beyond.[451]

In a May, 1981, CBC television interview, Bennett suggested that he believed his life had been threatened.[452] He moved to Australia, where he still lives.

Fortunately, Bennett had already spoken at length and it is worthwhile to quote him fully:

We knew the Americans had done a heavy shift of forces, although of course it would be referred to as routine exercises. We called them tanks, and you might get an argument from the military mind on this, because to me all large armored vehicles bearing guns are tanks, but they might be called something else, like heavy armored personnel carriers.

I'm not sure how the word got to the Canadian government, but certainly it was made abundantly clear that if the Quebec government fell or there was anything approaching a successful insurrection, the Americans would take steps — up to and including armed occupation — to protect their seaway interests ...

So a decision was made to bring Canadian tanks — again various kinds of heavy armored equipment — into a position that we could preserve national sovereignty if necessary.

And, simultaneously we had to dig into our limited manpower in an attempt to find out just what the CIA was up to. And that is only one of the untold stories of the October crisis.[453]

---

[450] Ibid. p. A4.
[451] Anon. (1973) "'Nothing to Say' in Ottawa," Toronto Star, Sept. 22, p. A1.
[452] J. Dubro (1991) Personal communication, August 25.
[453] T. Hazlitt (1973) "Ex-Spy Claims US Tanks Ready in Quebec Crisis," Toronto Star, Sept. 22, p. A4.

One lead from an unsolicited and unconfirmed source adds some further possibilities to Bennett's claim.[454] This account has it that the Canadian government was informed of US concern and military preparations by a US general who flew into the Canadian base at St. Hubert, just south of Montreal. The general informed the people in attendance that three US army divisions had been readied to invade Quebec to secure the region. Two were airborne and the third was an armoured force. The source of this account is supposedly a Canadian Air Force officer stationed at St. Hubert in October 1970. The commander of Canadian troops at St. Hubert at that time was Lieutenant General G.A. Turcot, now retired.[455] He has explicitly denied this story: "There wasn't any information about that sort of thing. I don't think they could have done it without our knowledge."[456]

Two days after the publication of the Bennett interview, various Canadian and US officials who had been party to the October Crisis denied Bennett's claims.[457] Donald MacDonald, Minister of Defence in 1970, said that he never heard about any US tanks on the border and he denied that the Canadian Government had moved armoured forces south of Ottawa in response to alleged US troop deployments. Rufus Smith, US deputy assistant Secretary of State for Canadian Affairs, assigned to the Ottawa Embassy in 1970, said that Bennett's claims were "utterly ridiculous," and the RCMP Commissioner said "they were the ravings of a disturbed mind." Robert Bourassa was quoted as saying, "Don't you think that it

---

[454] Personal communication, August 9, 1991.

[455] J. Castonguay (1980) *History of Canadian Forces Base Montreal and its Garrisons*, (publisher not identified).

[456] J. Picton (1991) "Is US Base Potential Threat to Canada?" *Toronto Star*, Dec. 1, p. A7.

[457] Anon. (1973) "Ottawa, Quebec, US Deny Ex-Spy Boss' Story of US Tanks at Border," *Toronto Star*, Sept. 24, pp. A1, A2.

Anon. (1973) "Officials Deny US Planned 1970 Quebec Invasion," *Globe and Mail*, Sept. 24, p. 4.

would have been pretty visible if American tanks were lined up at the Quebec border?"[458]

Two days later, in a CBC radio interview, Bennett himself retracted the statements attributed to him by the *Toronto Star*.[459] Bennett said that he did not know that he was being interviewed for publication and that the *Toronto Star* report was "totally untrue, mischievous, and irresponsible." He denied he had been instructed to change his story. But, according to the reporter taking Bennett's retraction, "he repeatedly skirted around a direct answer when asked if the matters in the reports had been discussed at all."[460]

Star interviewer, Hazlitt, however, stood by his report:

Hazlitt said he had introduced the subject of CIA infiltration in Montreal into the conversation, but Bennett had volunteered the other two items [that Canada had moved troops south of Ottawa to offset US deployments and that the United States had explicitly threatened a military occupation of Quebec], and confirmed all of them in intimate detail.[461]

Hazlitt said that he believed that Bennett was an honourable man but that something had transpired that compelled him to make a retraction. Hazlitt said that he had sought and found confirmation for Bennett's claims from contacts in the intelligence communities of both Canada and the United States, but that "he also was told that they would be denied as a matter of policy if brought to public attention."[462]

This defence of the Bennett interview was continued three days later by the *Toronto Star*'s executive editor, Mark Harrison.[463] He pointed to several examples of national government officials — even

[458] Anon. (1973) "Ottawa, Quebec, US Deny Ex-Spy Boss' Story of US Tanks at Border," *Toronto Star*, Sept. 24, p. A2.
[459] Anon. (1973) "Ex-Spy Catcher Denies US Had Plans to Invade," *Toronto Star*, Sept. 25, p. A2.
[460] Anon. (1973) "Officials Deny US Planned 1970 Quebec Invasion," *Globe and Mail*, Sept. 25, p. 3.
[461] Anon. (1973) "Ex-Spy Catcher Denies US had Plans to Invade," *Toronto Star*, Sept. 25, p. A2.
[462] Ibid.
[463] M. Harrison (1973) "The Official Denials are Only to be Expected," *Toronto Star*, Sept. 29, p. B2.

such trusted leaders as Dwight Eisenhower and Harold Macmillan — lying in the name of national interest. Harrison wrote:

Truth and honesty may be virtues in public life, but in government, alas, they often are considered subordinate to the national interest.

If it is deemed necessary to tell an outrageous lie in the interests of, say, national security, then it is done. Not with a blush of shame, but with a glow of patriotism.[464]

Mr. Harrison noted Hazlitt's reputation as an award-winning investigative reporter. He also quoted an unnamed Canadian military source to confirm Bennett's original story:

One former Canadian army officer told the *Star* that he was informed the Americans brought an armored brigade within striking distance of the St. Lawrence Seaway during the FLQ crisis, and that other US armored units were brought to a state of alert.

He said he was also informed that the Americans had a contingency plan under which US troops would move into southern Quebec if the government fell and was supplanted by a Marxist regime. He said the Canadian government was informed of this intent.[465]

At the time of Bennett's interview and the subsequent denials, he was under suspicion of being a double-agent for the Soviet Union. Indeed, Hazlitt initiated the interview to determine whether Bennett's medical discharge from the intelligence service was genuine or not. Bennett strongly denied any disloyalty on his part. Since that period, two sources have confirmed Bennett's integrity. Peter Wright, in *Spycatcher*, praised Bennett for being one Canadian intelligence officer who attempted to maintain independence from the CIA.[466] More recently, a biography of the CIA's top spycatcher revealed that the Agency had informed the RCMP in 1971 that Bennett was a mole. Apparently what initiated CIA suspicions was a remark by Bennett that he questioned the morality of Senator

---

[464] Ibid.

[465] Ibid.

[466] P. Wright (1987) *Spycatcher: The Candid Autobiography of a Senior Intelligence Officer*, Toronto: Stoddart.

Joseph McCarthy's methods. Bennett was cleared of all suspicions by both the CIA and the RCMP in 1977. [467]

Subsequent publications in Quebec may shed more light on US interests in Quebec nationalist movements. One is Jean-François Lisée's book, *In the Eye of the Eagle*, [468] which portrays US interest in Quebec separatism as passive and benign, even benevolent. The substance for that portrayal came from declassified US State Department documents. It would be interesting to determine if that declassification was in any way selective or designed. More obscure, but perhaps more provocative, is the small book *Une amitié bien particulière* (*A Unique Friendship*), [469] which documents the concerns and speculations of Jacques Ferron, a prominent Québécois nationalist, that Quebec politics were being manipulated to US ends.

If correct, Bennett's initial claim that the United States had prepared to intervene in Quebec in 1970 is not a minor point in Canadian-US relations and would have bearing on present concerns about Fort Drum. It deserves a full followup, even after two decades. Maybe Jim Bennett would now feel safe to speak freely, for publication, about those events. Other Canadian governmental and military personnel might be persuaded to speak on this matter, as might those on the US side. At the time of the Bennett interview, the *Toronto Star* did contact Pentagon sources. They said that military personnel and equipment are shifted every day for a variety of reasons. They said that it would be impossible to determine whether or not there had been troop movements near the northern

[467] T. Mangold (1991) *Cold Warrior: James Jesus Angleton, the CIA's Master Spy Hunter*, New York: Simon and Schuster.

Anon. (1991) "Wrong Canadian Spy Chaser Forced to Quit, Author Says," *Whig-Standard*, May 13, p. 4.

N.A. Shackleton (1991) "Machiavellian Tendencies" (review of *Cold Warrior*), *Whig-Standard Magazine*, Sept. 14, p. 22.

[468] J.-F. Lisée (1990) *In the Eye of the Eagle*, Toronto: Harper Collins.

[469] J. Ferron, edited by J. Grube (1990) *Une amitié bien particulière*, Montreal: Boreal.

border at that time. Finally, they said that they are forbidden to talk about it.[470]

It should not be impossible to determine if US troops and armour were assembled at the border in the autumn of 1970. A military force large enough to intervene in Quebec should have left some clues of its existence. The troops could not just drive around on private land or hide in state parks. They would have to have gathered at an established military base. There are three plausible sites for such a force: 1) Fort Drum, 2) Plattsburgh Air Force Base, or perhaps 3) the National Guard artillery range at Jericho, Vermont. The Jericho base is small and has few facilities. Plattsburgh, though large and complex, is exclusively an Air Force installation. It is exposed on all four sides to public view and is overlooked by a college campus. The sudden appearance of khaki uniforms and army tanks would have required public explanation. That leaves Fort Drum as the most reasonable possibility.

Armored forces assembled at Fort Drum in 1970 would not have been easily visible, and certainly would not have been lined up on the Quebec border, as Bourassa chided. However, they would have been within striking distance of Montreal. A force at Fort Drum would also explain Canadian movements of armour south of Ottawa. The local newspaper for the Fort Drum region did not report armoured forces at Fort Drum in October 1970.[471] But not all military activities at the base are reported in the local press. On the very day that Prime Minister Trudeau ordered troops into Montreal, a 175-man special forces group arrived at Fort Drum. This was Company D of the 10th Special Forces Group.[472] Civilians were warned to stay out of base training areas. It is not known what types of operations this unit specialized in or what missions it had undertaken before or after the October Crisis.

---

[470] T. Hazlitt (1973) "Ex-Spy Claims US Tanks Ready in Quebec Crisis," *Toronto Star*, Sept. 22, p. A4.
[471] J. Picton (1991) "Is US Base Potential Threat to Canada?" *Toronto Star*, Dec. 1, p. A7.
[472] Anon. (1970) "Special Forces Unit will Train at Drum" *Watertown Daily Times*, Oct. 16, p.10.

If the Bennett interview is correct, the movement of US troops to the border and their preparations for an attack into Canada prematurely gave away the plan and allowed Canadian authorities time to deploy counterforce. If so, then it is reasonable to presume that US military planners would take steps to make sure that does not happen a second time. Now that Fort Drum is the permanent garrison for an assault division and now that the command and heavy equipment for a reserve armoured division are also in place, there will be no convoys or stockpiling to be detected. If the various reports about "Task Force Revolt" are correct, then it is reasonable to presume that US military planners will not allow any contingency plans for Canada to be widely known, even within inner Washington circles. Those mistakes will not happen a second time.

There may have already been a second time. Two quite independent, unsolicited and unconfirmed sources have related accounts of the United States preparing military contingency forces for the 1980 Quebec Referendum on sovereignty-association. One source, claiming first-hand information from Canadian military personnel, said that US and Canadian military units had been readied near Montreal on the eve of the referendum.[473] The other source, claiming first-hand information from a US Embassy staff member, wrote:

In the Summer of 1984, I was about to enter my second year at McGill and I was living for the Summer in Ottawa, working at Mags and Fags magazine store on Elgin St. There was a regular customer, an American, probably in his 30s, who stopped to chat with me at the store ... He said he worked at the US Embassy there and was soon going to be transferred. We got to talking about Montreal and he talked a lot about the usual things — how cosmopolitan it was, the French "influence," etc — and when the conversation turned political, and I said something about Québécois nationalism, he said that the US had mobilised troops south of the border and naval ships off the coast just prior to the referendum in 1980, something he termed as a "precaution" or "just in case." He said it matter-of-factly, in a way that showed he clearly assumed that these are the kinds of precautions one (i.e. the US) takes in these kinds of historical

---

[473] Personal communication, March 2, 1992.

moments. He was not shocked by this. I was. I really didn't know what to say, especially as I was sure that — if he really did work at the US Embassy — he really should never have told me that. Frankly, it kind of killed the conversation because I felt he had made a mistake that might somehow get me into trouble. He came into the store several times after that, but we didn't talk much more again. If only it had happened a few years later, I might have grilled him with questions.[474]

WHO IS HENRY GABLINGER?

It may be that the origins of recent developments at Fort Drum, if they are hostile towards Canada, began someplace in the Kennedy or Nixon administrations and have had subsequent revival in the Reagan-Bush administration. Two decades ago, during the Nixon administration, the Kingston *Whig-Standard* reprinted an interview with a Mr. Henry Gablinger. The headline was, "Take Over Canada? A Friendly Southern Neighbour Looks North."[475]

The interview was done by a Mr. John Samson for the US newspaper *The Examiner*. Richard Preston concluded that the interview must have been fraudulent since "no such American periodical had ever existed."[476] In fact, there were several US newspapers with the name *Examiner*.[477] However, the interview is nevertheless in doubt. According to a search by the Columbia University School of Journalism, there was only one US journalist by the name of John Samson in that period. He was a Nieman Fellow at Harvard in 1960.[478] When shown the interview and asked about it, John Samson disavowed it as his work and added that he always wrote under the byline of Jack Samson.[479]

---

[474] Personal communication, May 12, 1992.

[475] J. Samson (1971) "Take Over Canada? A Friendly Southern Neighbour Looks North," *Whig-Standard*, June 7, p. 6.

[476] R.A. Preston (1977) *The Defence of the Undefended Border: Planning for War in North America 1867-1939*, Montreal: McGill-Queen's University Press, p. 2.

[477] Anon. (1990) *Gale Directory of Publication and Broadcast Media* (vol. 3), New York: Gale Research, pp. 3334-3335.

[478] Personal communication, May 7, 1991.

[479] J. Samson (1991), Personal communication, June 2.

The person interviewed, Henry Gablinger, was described as a resources expert and adviser to Richard Nixon. However, there is no record of a Henry Gablinger in the Nixon administration: not in the US government catalogues of the Nixon Administration's staff,[480] not in *Who's Who in America*,[481] not in the *New York Times Index*.[482] So it may be that "Henry Gablinger" is a pseudonym for some other prominent adviser to Richard Nixon, or it may be that the entire interview is a fabrication designed by persons unknown for purposes unknown. In style, it has much of the mocking quality commonly used in US discussions of Canadian concerns about US military power.

In any case, the argument was made that the United States is going to need Canadian resources and that it will take them by treaty or by force. "It is not really a question of how," said Mr. Gablinger. "We have the means to conquer Canada. It is a question of when." The argument is all very reasonable:

Granted that Canada has been our peaceful neighbor for several hundred years (sic) and that we have shared a border from Maine to Washington without incident. But life in the international jungle is rough and if the US is to make it to the year 2000, it needs the fantastic natural resources that sit just a few miles above its border.[483]

"It is all very simple," said Gablinger. "Just look at the figures." He then went on to cite demographic and resource statistics, with a focus on thirty-three critical resources, the foremost being energy and water. Canada has the resources the United States needs and if resource exports are restricted or a shortage occurs, they will simply be taken. Said the report:

The US has never been shy about taking what it wants in the past. And driven to the wall, it will do the same with Canada.

[480] Office of the Federal Register (1971) *United States Government Organization Manual 1971/72*, Washington, DC: Government Printing Office.
[481] Anon. (1973) *Who's Who in America, 1969-1973, with Index to All Volumes*, Chicago: Marquis Who's Who.
[482] Anon. (1969-1972) *The New York Times Index*, New York: New York Times Corp.
[483] J. Samson (1971) "Take Over Canada? A Friendly Southern Neighbour Looks North," *Whig-Standard*, June 7, p. 6.

"Actually we are being very nice about it," said Gablinger. "We have offered all kinds of deals to the Canadians such as the Continental Energies Program which would unite all the resources in North America into one common pool. If they don't accept it, we'll just have to force it on them ...

"As the President said to me, 'We're going to have to start calling in our IOUs and Canada's the one deepest in debt to us.'"[484]

The interview went on to report that international observers saw many small signs of growing tensions between the United States and Canada, "tensions that will eventually either erupt into a war in which Canada will be humiliatingly defeated or smolder into Canada's complete submission to any US demands."[485]

That was 1971. At the time, the interview may have appeared ridiculous, even comic if that was the intention. But with twenty-year hind-sight, it seems to be prophetic, at least of the Canada-US Free Trade Agreement, particularly sections on energy resource pooling. Article 904 of the Agreement guarantees the United States a fixed proportion of the total supply of Canadian energy resources, even should Canada experience energy shortages.[486]

Ironically, the new base at Fort Drum contributed significantly to the demand to expand Canadian natural gas supply capabilities to the United States. Documents released by TransCanada Pipelines for the local public hearings on laying the pipeline across the Thousand Islands state that the massive expansion of Fort Drum created the gas demands that necessitate this new pipeline, which is one of the largest gas pipeline expansions in Canadian history.[487]

The free trade debates also brought focus on US interests in Canadian fresh water resources. As the United States depletes and contaminates its own fresh water, at a time when irrigation, drought and urban growth in the dry southwest are increasing, it is inevitable

---

[484] Ibid.

[485] Ibid.

[486] M.M. Bowker (1988) On Guard for Thee: An Independent Review of the Free Trade Agreement, Hull, Que.: Voyageur.

[487] C. Graham (1990) "Canadian Users Must Pay for Gas Pipeline to US," Whig-Standard, Nov. 7, p. 18.

that Canada will be seen as a natural and rightful source of water. [488] A sign of US interest in Canadian water resources is the recent US financing and legal intervention in the Rafferty-Alameda dams in Saskatchewan. When the Canadian federal Department of the Environment tried to halt construction for the mandatory environmental impact study, the US Army Corps of Engineers intervened in the court proceedings:

A spokesman for the US Army Corps of Engineers declared on Oct. 19 that, whether or not a federal environmental review finds the project acceptable, Saskatchewan must build it exactly as planned. The US, he pointed out, has already paid Saskatchewan $17 million (US) out of the $50 million it plans to pay the province.[489]

US funding and intervention are for a dam that is supposedly for irrigating Canadian farms. The Rafferty-Alameda dams and the Oldman River Dam in Alberta all make little sense for Canadian water management but fit very nicely into longstanding US plans for continental water diversion from Canada to the United States. Simon Reisman, Canada's principle free trade negotiator, was an advisor for the United States' Grand Canal water diversion project.[490]

Despite subsequent evidence of US interest in Canadian energy and water resources, the Gablinger interview is perplexing. Because its source and intent are unknown, not too much can be made of it. It is clear in retrospect that its demographic and resource use projections were quite inaccurate, always overestimating US demands. However, as a true expression of US strategic thinking, or perhaps as a satire of it, the easy and confident threat of force in the Gablinger interview is frightening for its reasonableness.

---

[488] D. Bueckert. (1990) "Canada, US Could Clash Over Water, Expert Says," *Whig-Standard*, April 12, p. 10.
[489] D. Orchard and M. Repo (1990) "Dam Project Part of a Scheme to Divert Canadian Water to the States" (letter), *Whig-Standard*, Nov. 2, p. 5.
[490] Ibid.

CHAPTER 10

STEADY MARCH

The steady march of events and history does not stop. New developments occur on a continual basis and the directions these new developments take allow some retrospective judgement on whether or not earlier concerns about Fort Drum, or US military preparations generally, were warranted. Unfortunately, there is little evidence that earlier concerns were unwarranted.

OPERATIONS JUST CAUSE AND DESERT STORM

Since the original research on Fort Drum in the autumn of 1989,[491] the United States has undertaken two major military interventions in Third World regions that had been discussed as target sites for the Fort Drum forces. However, Fort Drum's light infantry brigades were not deployed to Operation Just Cause in Panama in 1989 nor to Operation Desert Storm in the Persian Gulf in 1991. Failure to

---

[491] F.W. Rudmin (1989) "Offensive Light Infantry Forces at Fort Drum, New York: Why Should Canadians Care?" *Queen's Quarterly*, vol. 96 (no. 4), pp. 886-917.

participate in either of these conflicts reinforces suspicion that such conflicts are indeed not Fort Drum's true mission.

The light infantry forces for the pre-Christmas surprise attack on Panama's national capital came from Fort Ord, not from Fort Drum.[492] On the day of the attack, December 20, Fort Drum was beset by winter weather, with the temperature falling well below freezing and predictions calling for snow squalls.[493] When 2,000 light infantry reinforcements were sent to Panama on December 22, again, they came from Fort Ord, not Fort Drum.[494] However, units from Fort Drum were not altogether absent from the Panama campaign. There was a military police company from Fort Drum in Panama at the time of Operation Just Cause.[495] They had been sent there in October to help with security at US Canal Zone military bases.

For the Persian Gulf War, once again Fort Drum's light infantry were not deployed while Fort Ord's were. Since US troop deployments to the Gulf took place during the preceding summer and autumn, Fort Drum's bad weather cannot be taken as the excuse. The explanation given for the absence of Fort Drum forces was:

Their ability to get to the scene quickly was not needed as the United States built up its forces over a five-month period. And without tanks, they weren't going to be able to overcome Iraqi fortifications and expel the invaders from Kuwait.[496]

Of course, this is in contradiction to the fact that Fort Ord's light infantry went to the Gulf War.[497]

In fact, the Persian Gulf War was an excellent, perhaps an ideal, scenario to demonstrate the rapid deployment of light infantry

[492] Anon. (1989) "US Dispatches 9,000 Soldiers to Canal Zone," *Watertown Daily Times*, Dec. 20, p. 1.
[493] *Watertown Daily Times*, Dec. 20, p. 1.
[494] Anon. (1989) "Panama Street Fights Continue," *Watertown Daily Times*, Dec. 23, p. 1, 7.
[495] F.A. Pound (1989) "Fort Drum Troops in Panama 'Safe' So Far," *Watertown Daily Times*, Dec. 22, p. 22.
[496] J.D. Salant (1991) "The War that Never Was," *Post-Standard* (Syracuse), March 25, p. A4.
[497] A. Emory (1991) "Fort Drum Escapes Ax: Panel Votes to Keep it, Despite Low Rating," *Watertown Daily Times*, June 8, pp. 30, 26.

forces. Fort Drum's 10th Division supposedly could have, and hence probably should have, engaged its "official" mission as a rapid-deployment, preemptive, Third World intervention force. If one or more divisions of light infantry had flown into Kuwait the weekend before Iraq invaded, they might have prevented the entire Gulf War, with all of its death and destruction. The deployment of light infantry to the Persian Gulf had long been predicted. Their readiness for that scenario had been used as part of the very rationale for their creation.

Indeed, in 1984 there was discussion of making light infantry capable of responding to anticipated invasions of the Gulf oil states by armoured forces.[498] It seems clear that the United States did know that the invasion was going to occur. A CBC television documentary showed that just one month before Iraq's invasion of Kuwait, US forces were rehearsing in the California desert for war against Iraq.[499] But, of course, preemptive forces would not have been sent if the United States had intentionally encouraged the invasion, as was argued by the documentary and more recently by US presidential candidate Ross Perot.[500]

Fort Drum did not send any light infantry combat troops to the Persian Gulf War. As with the attack on Panama, however, Fort Drum did contribute some auxiliary units: supply, police, and air ambulance vehicles and personnel.[501] These units did not fly out of Fort Drum in a display of rapid deployment capability. The helicopters were flown to New Jersey for disassembly and packing for shipment overseas. The wheeled vehicles were put on a freight train.

[498] M.R. Gordon (1984) "The Charge of the Light Infantry: Army Plans Forces for Third World Conflicts," *National Journal*, vol. 16, May 19, p. 968.
[499] N. Docherty (producer) (1991) "Oil War," CBC documentary aired on Feb. 19.
[500] L. Diebel (1992) "Perot Accuses Bush of Deal with Iraq," *Toronto Star*, Oct. Oct. 20, p. A18.
[501] T. Wilber (1990) "Army Deploys Drum Vehicles: Copters Part of Desert Shield," *Watertown Daily Times*, Aug. 29, pp. 32, 26.

Operation Just Cause in Panama and Operation Desert Storm in the Persian Gulf might have demonstrated that Fort Drum forces could and would be used as US military and governmental officials have been saying, for rapid deployment to Third World regions. The fact that they were not sent reinforces concern that their true mission is elsewhere.

MILITARY MAKE-WORK

However, Fort Drum's light infantry have been sent on several so-called "humanitarian" missions. Because of the frequency of these deployments, even when other forces were more convenient and more cost-effective, it appears that the Army is engaged in a public relations program to justify the Fort Drum expansion and to establish a reputation for Fort Drum's assault troops as a humanitarian aid corps, albeit dressed over in camouflage.

For example, in December 1991, 350 troops were sent to the US naval base at Guantanamo, Cuba, to help manage Haitian refugees detained there until deportation.[502] The troops were part of a "joint task force" expected to be in Cuba for 90 days. However, the populist, libertarian newspaper *Spotlight* reported that the troops did not take weapons with them as they flew from Griffiss Air Force Base.[503] An unnamed officer from Fort Drum said that weapons for the Fort Drum troops may have been on flights from Stewart Air Force Base:

The day after the 10th Mountain Division troops left for Guantanamo, three Air Force transport aircraft were dispatched from Stewart Air Force Base in Newburgh, N.Y., supposedly carrying donated food and clothing for the Haitian refugees.

However, the aircraft operation was cloaked in secrecy with the press denied permission to accompany the supplies to the naval base due to "weight

---

[502] M. Smith (1991) "350 Soldiers of 10th Mountain Division Heading for Cuba," *Watertown Daily Times*, Dec. 24, p. 27.
[503] M. Blair (1992) "Castro Said on Way Out,"*Spotlight*, Jan. 27, pp. 11, 17.

restrictions." Reporters at Guantanamo were not even allowed to see the humanitarian supplies when they landed....[504]

The newspaper surmised that the whole operation was part of military preparations to support a new Cuban government following the eventual fall of Castro.

The first major deployment of Fort Drum's forces, with full public relations fanfare, was to help civilians in Florida cope with extensive property damage caused by Hurricane Andrew and to help President Bush cope with extensive election damage caused by his failure to respond to domestic problems. Hurricane Andrew struck in August 1992 and devastated communities around Homestead Air Force Base near Miami.[505] After public complaint about government unresponsiveness, Florida's 3,000 National Guardsmen and approximately 7,000 federal troops were ordered to give aid.[506] Then, an additional 5,000 troops were promised,[507] and further deployments would bring the total to 20,000.[508] With all of these forces and all of these men, Bush still couldn't get elected again. But the Pentagon itself put together a package of public goodwill for its fight against proposed base closures and budget cuts announced at about that time.[509]

Fort Drum troops were among those deployed to Florida. On August 31, troops began going by bus to Griffiss Air Force Base to board military transports and chartered commercial jets.[510] One C-141 took ten soldiers and five vehicles, another took twenty-eight soldiers and fourteen vehicles. It was estimated that 400-450 troops

---

[504] Ibid., p. 11.

[505] Anon. (1992) "Hurricane Andrew Wallops S. Florida," *Watertown Daily Times*, Aug. 24, p. 1.

[506] Anon. (1992) "Bush Orders Troops to Florida," *New York Times*, Aug. 28, p. A1.
Anon. (1992) "Military Aid Lands on Florida," *Watertown Daily Times*, Aug. 29, pp. 1, 7.
Anon. (1992) "First of 6000 Troops and 1000 Marines Arrive," *New York Times*, Aug. 29, p. 11.

[507] Anon. (1992) "Bush Promises 5,000 More Troops," *New York Times*, Aug. 30, p. 122.

[508] Anon. (1992) "20,000 Troops Might Be Sent," *New York Times*, Aug. 31, p. A10.

[509] Anon. (1992) "Pentagon Set for Deeper Budget Cuts," *Watertown Daily Times*, Aug. 30, pp. 1, 9.

[510] M. Smith (1992) "Soldiers Head for Florida to Aid Hurricane Victims," *Watertown Daily Times*, Aug. 31, pp. 28, 24.

would go per day, until a total of 7,000 were deployed. After two days of airlift deployment from Griffiss Air Force Base using C-141s, C-5As, and chartered 747s, 280 vehicles, twenty cargo trailers and 630 soldiers had reached Florida.[511] Five days after deployment began, 2,561 Fort Drum troops had made it to Florida and fifty railroad cars were waiting at the base to carry vehicles and cargo south.[512] Eventually, between August 31 and September 10, 4,844 Fort Drum troops reached Florida.[513] Thus, even on a mission totally within the continental United States, with the benefit of transport by rail and commercial jets, and without the handicap of winter weather and without need for weaponry or battlefield logistics, the deployment was less than rapid. Certainly it was far from the deployment rate of 2,500 troops per day originally expected of a light infantry division. Most of the criticisms of Fort Drum as a rapid deployment base were borne out.

The assault troops stayed in Florida for about two months. Their mission entailed no martial law or police duties. Wrote the *New York Times*, "Troops stationed there tell of duties that are straight out of the *Boy Scout Handbook*."[514] For example, sorting canned goods, sweeping parking lots, moving furniture, cleaning debris from homeowners' yards, doing laundry for homeless people, running a soup kitchen. The *Times* article showed a picture of a soldier carrying groceries for a woman in a wheel chair. "We're infantry soldiers, and we're used to doing that job," said one soldier, "but this is something totally new and different for us."[515]

The late start, the slow arrival, the make-work nature of the activities, all argue that this was a public relations exercise. And it has yet to be made public what this exercise cost. In the midst of

---

[511] K. Burton (1992) "Another 10th Battalion Expects Orders for Florida Relief Effort," *Watertown Daily Times*, Sept. 2, pp. 30, 26.
[512] F.A. Pound (1992) "Drum GIs Clean Up in Florida," *Watertown Daily Times*, Sept. 4, pp. 32, 28.
[513] L. Rohter (1992) "Mountain Troops Helping in Florida," *New York Times*, Sept. 11, p. A20.
[514] Ibid.
[515] Ibid.

the deployment to Florida, there was a report from Washington headlined "Northern New York Faces Uphill Struggle in Efforts to Avert Military Base Closing."[516] The day that Fort Drum's commander returned from Florida, the Secretary of the Army held a teleconference explaining that budget justification now requires the Army to do more for the good of the country.[517] He pointed to the Florida deployment and AIDS research as prime examples. However, he emphasized that the Army must do these side jobs "while not compromising its primary objectives of staying lethal and ready."[518]

The Florida humanitarian mission was just a warm-up. The next deployment of Fort Drum's assault troops was Operation Restore Hope in Somalia. As with the Florida mission, publicity was maximized. As with the Florida mission, the inadequacies of Fort Drum as a base for rapid airlift deployment were evident. It was also evident that the US Marines were easily coping with the situation and that the Fort Drum forces were redundant. It was a mission of salvation, not only the salvation of starving African children, but also the salvation of Fort Drum.

General Colin Powell, Chairman of the Joint Chiefs of Staff, said that Operation Restore Hope is "a paid political advertisement" for the military.[519] A *Washington Post* exposé read:

.... a successful mission could yield a public relations bonanza at just the right time .... "I'd be lying if I said that never occurred to us," said Brig. Gen. Thomas V. Draude, chief of public affairs for the Marine Corps. .... It is a sense that is shared by all the services, as they seek to showcase their capabilities and usefulness at a time when Congress is under intense pressure to produce post-Cold War defense savings.[520]

---

[516] A. Emory (1992) "Northern New York Faces Uphill Struggle in Efforts to Avert Military Base Closing," *Watertown Daily Times*, Sept. 3, pp. 34, 28.
[517] A. Emory (1992) "Non-War Role Said Big Part of New Army," *Watertown Daily Times*, Oct. 10, p. 30.
[518] Ibid.
[519] J. Lancaster (1992) "For Marine Corps, Somalia Operation Offers New Esprit: Mission Could Generate 'Good News' as Service Confronts Shrinking Budgets," *Washington Post*, Dec. 6, p. A34.
[520] Ibid.

The Army apparently considered Fort Drum to be its highest public relations priority.

On December 2, 1992, a US-sponsored resolution was unanimously adopted by the UN calling for a multilateral military intervention in Somalia.[521] The Pentagon said that the Marine Corps and elements of the 10th Division would take part. The plan called for a 1,800 Marine landing force to be followed by 16,000 Marines flown in from California. The 10th Division was to follow[522] with a force of 5,000 troops[523] destined for missions in Baidoa, Belet Uen, Hoddur and Gailalassi.[524]

One week later, the Marines landed in Somalia's capital.[525] That same day, Fort Drum forces began their deployment, with attack helicopters flying to New Jersey for disassembly and shipment by sea to Somalia.[526] Cargo trailers, bull dozers, communication equipment and 350 vehicles were loaded onto 82 railcars ready for transport to the coast and shipment to Somalia. Loading conditions were well below freezing and icy. As critics of light infantry had predicted, the helicopters and vehicles were not amenable to airlift deployment. As critics of Fort Drum had predicted, bad weather did hamper deployment.[527] A snow storm with high winds delayed

---

[521] P. Lewis (1992) "Key U.N. Members Agree to U.S. Force in Somalia Mission," New York Times, Dec. 3, p. 1.

[522] M.R. Gordon (1992) "Mission to Somalia: U.N. Backs a Somalia Force as Bush Vows a Swift Exist; Pentagon Sees Longer Stay," New York Times, Dec. 4, p. 1.

M.R. Gordon (1992) "Mission to Somalia: U.S. is Sending Large Force as Warning to Somali Clans, " New York Times, Dec. 5, p. 5.

[523] J. Lancaster (1992) "U.S. Plans Staging Base, Mogadishu Port, Airport to be Improved," Washington Post, Dec. 4, p. A1.

[524] M.R. Gordon (1992) "Mission to Somalia: U.S. is Sending Large Force as Warning to Somali Clans, " New York Times, Dec. 5, p. 5.

[525] J. Perlez (1992) "Mission to Somalia: U.S. Forces Arrive in Somalia on Mission to Aid the Starving, " New York Times, Dec. 9, p. A1.

[526] M. Smith and C. Noble (1992) "Chief Says: I Don't Know When 10th Will Go," Watertown Daily Times, Dec. 9, pp. 32, 28.

[527] C. Noble (1992) "Troops of 10th Flying Friday," Watertown Daily Times, Dec. 10, pp. 34, 28.

transport to Griffiss Air Force Base[528] and flights were suspended for 24 hours.[529]

After one week of deployment, 400 troops had reached Somalia and 1,200 vehicles had gone by train to New Jersey for shipment to Africa.[530] After two weeks of deployment, few light infantry had reached Africa:

The slow and spotty nature of the deployment — so far only about 700 troops from Fort Drum with fewer than 100 vehicles are in Somalia — is due almost entirely to a "bottleneck" of flights to Somalia.[531]

Critics of light infantry had predicted that target country airport facilities would not be adequate for the large numbers of military transport aircraft needed for light infantry rapid deployment. As predicted, Fort Drum's own airfield, despite a $60,000,000 expansion, was inadequate for transoceanic transport aircraft and played no role in the deployment.[532] After three weeks of deployment, one fifth of the 10th Mountain Division had made it to Africa.[533] As critics had predicted, the Marines were capable of handling any of the missions that light infantry might assume. After more than three weeks in Africa, Fort Drum's light infantry still had done nothing. "Most soldiers here said they had not seen any starving Somalis, and many have had almost no contact with the indigenous population."[534] Four weeks into deployment, nearly 3,500 light infantry had reached Africa[535] and had begun relieving Marines of airport guard duties and food shipment protection.[536]

---

[528] C. Noble (1992) "Troops Departure Delayed by Storm Over Rome Base," *Watertown Daily Times*, Dec. 11, pp. 34, 28.

[529] M. Smith (1992) "First Drum Troops Head to Somalia,"*Watertown Daily Times*, Dec. 12, pp. 30, 26.

[530] M. Smith (1992) "Largest Group Yet is Headed for Somalia," *Watertown Daily Times*, Dec. 16, pp. 30, 26.

[531] C. Noble (1992) "Fort Drum Commander Arrives in Somalia Today," *Watertown Daily Times*, Dec. 22, p. 28.

[532] M. Smith (1992) "Fort Drum's Wheeler Sack Not Used for Deployment," *Watertown Daily Times*, Dec. 24, p. 29.

[533] M. Smith (1992) "Deployment Continues as Planned," *Watertown Daily Times*, Dec. 31, pp. 32, 28.

[534] D.B. Beeson (1993) "10th Division Soldiers Greet Bush in Somalia," *Watertown Daily Times*, Jan. 2, p. 30.

[535] M. Smith (1993) "4 Planes Head for Somalia," *Watertown Daily Times*, Jan. 6, pp. 30, 26.

[536] D.B. Beeson (1993) "More Food Getting Through with Help of Drum GIs," *Watertown Daily Times*, Jan. 4, pp. 28, 24.

One month after the deployment began and 4,000 of Fort Drum's light infantry had reached Africa, the Pentagon announced that there was decreasing need for troops and that some were returning.[537]

There is little doubt that Somalia required and benefitted from foreign military intervention. There is little doubt that the US military can move personnel and equipment from any point on the globe to any point on the globe. The doubt is that the selection of Fort Drum troops for a humanitarian mission in Africa served public relations more than it did military rationale. The public relations emphasis of the exercise was highlighted when the Army refused to allow a local reporter to accompany the deployment because he had written about troops disgruntled with a command decision.[538] Another article entitled "10th Mountain Division 'Double Halo' May be Drum's Savior" began with the observation, "The tragedy in Somalia may turn out to be a blessing in disguise for Fort Drum."[539] The disguise is rather thin. The public relations benefits were predictable.

DEEP WOODS

Fort Drum is not the only unusual military preparation on the Canadian border. At a time when the United States has a clear surplus of military bases and is closing many of them,[540] land for a completely new base is being acquired on the Maine-New Brunswick border. Called Deep Woods, the base will encompass three-quarters of a million acres, extending from the coast at Calais

---

[537] I. Stewart (1993) "35 Drum Soldiers Return from Somalia," *Watertown Daily Times*, Jan. 10, p. A9.

[538] Anon. (1992) "Army Says Times Reporter Can't Follow Drum Troops," *Watertown Daily Times*, Dec. 9, p. 28.

[539] A. Emory (1992) "10th Mountain Division 'Double Halo' May be Drum's Savior," *Watertown Daily Times*, Dec. 15, p. 26.

[540] G. Ifill (1991) "35 More Bases Considered for Closing," *New York Times*, June 1, p. 7.

up Route 9.[541] The base is being built on the timberland of the Champion Paper Company; the lease will run for 30 years.

Ostensibly, Deep Woods will be a Maine National Guard base, but it will be under Pentagon command and used for training a variety of forces, both active and reserve. Plans call for year-round facilities for thousands of troops. Units training there will include combat engineers, special forces and Marines. As at Fort Drum, night assault practice will be a speciality. Civilian security police will also be preparing at Deep Woods for operations to control civilian populations. US-trained security police are responsible for much of the state terrorism and torture in Latin America.[542]

The acquisition of land for the base and the plans for its development have been very much out of the public eye. The citizens of Maine were not aware of any of this until it was mentioned by an environmentalist candidate for state governor, Nancy Oden, running for the Common Sense Party. She lives just a few miles from the new base and learned about it only by chance.

If it is plausible that Fort Drum's preparations are directed at central Canada, then it is plausible that Deep Woods' preparations are directed at the Atlantic provinces. If the separation of Quebec is successfully achieved, then the Atlantic provinces would be the quickest candidates for annexation by the United States. At any rate, that is Patrick Buchanan's opinion and hope:

If Quebec secedes, New Brunswick, Prince Edward Island, Nova Scotia and Newfoundland would be separated from Ottawa by 1,000 miles. With their ties to New England, the Atlantic provinces could choose to apply for statehood.[543]

Certainly, the economic vulnerability of the Atlantic provinces is greatest, especially if they are geographically cut off from the rest of Canada. Polls have shown the Atlantic provinces to be least

---

[541] This information came from Nancy Oden, personal communication, October 6, 1991.

[542] J. Roberts (1992) "The US Army School of the Americas," *Catholic Worker*, vol. 59 (no. 1), Jan.-Feb., pp. 5-6.
   J. Nelson-Pallmeyer (1989) *War Against the Poor*, Maryknoll, NY: Orbis.

[543] P. Buchanan (1990) "Quebec: The Next Nation?," *The Bangor Daily News*, May 2.

resistant to the possibility of statehood. The Gallup Poll released May 3, 1990, shows that 19% of Maritimers thought that Canada would break up, compared to 15% for the other English provinces.[544] The Gallup Poll released June 7, 1990, shows that 22% of Maritimers would approve of their provinces joining the United States, compared to 10% for the other English provinces.[545] The former Nova Scotia premier, John Buchanan, has said that the region would have no choice but to join the United States.[546] More recently, a US magazine has cited Canadian sources for the claim: "Two provinces, Manitoba and New Brunswick, have inquired about joining the United States."[547] Only Manitoba denied the report.

The US Army claims that it needs Deep Woods in order to prepare to fight the former Soviet Union. The terrain and climate may be similar to those in some parts of Russia, but they are identical to those in the Atlantic provinces. Maybe there is a realistic scenario for US troops and security police to intervene in Russia. Or maybe the United States needs another military base, if the existing facilities — 4,000 according to the *Washington Post* [548] — are not enough. Maybe it truly is only a coincidence that they are now building another new army base on the Canadian border. As with Fort Drum, these explanations are curious if not unbelievable. It might be enlightening to discover any US government agencies, officials, or lobbyists who were instrumental in the planning or the advocacy of both Fort Drum and Deep Woods.

---

[544] Anon. (1990) "Gallup Poll," *Whig-Standard*, p. 8.
[545] Anon. (1990) "Canadians Set Against Joining US, Poll Finds" *Whig-Standard*, June 7, p. 10.
[546] Anon. (1990) "US an Option if Quebec Separates, Buchanan Says," *Toronto Star*, April 19, p. A1.
[547] Anon. (1991) "Provinces Eye Link with US, Pair Say," *Whig-Standard*, Sept. 15, p. A12.
[548] M. Weisskopf (1985) "Community Happily Anticipates Army Invasion," *Washington Post*, May 27, p. A3.

FORT DRUM SAVED

One final curious development has been the slating of Fort Drum for closure, and then one week later, a reversal of that decision. The United States has long had surplus military bases. With decreased threat from communism and Russia and with mounting budget deficits in Washington, pressures to close unneeded military bases have become irresistible.

This is not a totally new development. In 1983, just before the creation of the new Fort Drum, a special commission advising President Reagan recommended the closing of fifty US military bases, for an annual savings of $2,000,000,000.[549] In 1988, even as Fort Drum was still being constructed, a Congressional panel proposed closing 86 military bases for a savings of $5,000,000,000.[550] In 1989, exactly at the time of the attack on Panama City, there was discussion of eliminating the 6th Light Infantry Division in Alaska and the 25th Light Infantry Division in Hawaii because military threats to Alaska and Korea had so diminished.[551]

In the spring of 1991, the United States convened a Defense Base Closure and Realignment Commission to consider the closure of forty-three bases. It was anticipated that any decisions to close military bases would be opposed by intense lobbying pressures from political and military interests. The Commission was therefore constructed and mandated to be resistant to those pressures. It was chaired by Congressman James Courter, a military expert and politically conservative who was soon to retire from public office. The Commission also included a former Secretary of the Navy, a

---

[549] Ibid.

[550] Anon. (1988) "Panel Proposes Closing 86 Military Bases," *Watertown Daily Times*, Dec. 29, pp. 1, 11.

[551] A. Emory (1989) "Martin Predicts Troop Cutback in Korea; Opposes Axing of Two Infantry Division," *Watertown Daily Times*, Dec. 21, pp. 1, 12.

retired Air Force general, a former ambassador, a former chair of the American Stock Exchange and others of similar status.[552]

On June 1, this nonpartisan panel of military experts announced that it had identified more bases that seem to have insufficient military rationale to justify continued operations. In that list was Fort Drum.[553] Also listed for closure were Griffiss Air Force Base and Plattsburgh Air Force Base. With three major bases in one Congressional district slated for closing, Congressman David Martin was sought by US national press for comment. In marked contrast to other Congressmen who had much less at stake, Martin was surprisingly confident: "The Commission, if they're doing their job, have to look into these kinds of things."[554] One week later, the Commission took Fort Drum and Griffiss Air Force Base off the list.[555]

The explanations for this decision continue to display the inconsistencies that make official explanations for Fort Drum incredible and suspect. It appears that the Army made some insistent but unexplained claim that it needed to keep Fort Drum, and the Commission acquiesced. The Army had some plan, and the Commission felt that it should not constrain military planning:

Commissioner William Ball, 3rd, a former Navy secretary, said the commission "should not tie the president's hands" by threatening Forts Drum and Richardson's strategic importance. He favored retaining both rather than making a decision for the Army.[556]

---

[552] G. Ifill (1991) "35 More Bases Considered for Closing," *New York Times*, June 1, p. 7.
[553] Ibid.
B. Gellman (1991) "Military Base Closing List Expanded," *Washington Post*, June 1, p. A4.
[554] Ibid.
A. Emory (1991) "Drum Not Seen as Likely Target of Base-Closing Panel," *Watertown Daily Times*, June 1, pp. 30, 26.
[555] A. Emory (1991) "Fort Drum Escapes Ax: Panel Votes to Keep it, Despite Low Rating," *Watertown Daily Times*, June 8, pp. 30, 28.
G. Ifill (1991) "Debate Intensifies as Talks Continue on Military Base Closing," *New York Times*, June 8, p. 8.
[556] A. Emory (1991) "Fort Drum Escapes Ax: Panel Votes to keep it, Despite Low Rating," *Watertown Daily Times*, June 8, p. 28.

Commissioner James Smith, a former staff aide on the Senate Armed Services Committee, said that they should not be closing "fighting" bases like Fort Drum but should be looking to close "training" bases.[557] In the end, the Commissioners voted six-to-one to retain Fort Drum. Furthermore, they declined the option of reconsidering Fort Drum for closure in 1993.

However, by objective analyses, measuring performance and capability against avowed mission, Fort Drum should have been closed. The independent Army Auditing Agency, examining the comparative cost-effectiveness of military bases, placed Fort Drum at the bottom of the list of bases under consideration. One of the principle reasons for being given the worst rating was the lack of space for maneuvres.[558] Commissioner Calloway referred to this as Fort Drum's "limited" training capability. However, despite the present overcrowding, it was announced that Fort Drum might soon be receiving another full brigade.[559] Congress has also approved construction of a "mock urban terrain project" to better prepare troops for fighting in cities.[560]

A more dramatic inconsistency was that Fort Drum was being preferred over Fort Ord. Commissioner Calloway, Secretary of the Army in the Ford Administration, is considered to be a friend of Fort Drum because it was he who authorized the change in designation from Camp Drum to Fort Drum.[561] Nevertheless, he was appalled — "it makes you cry," he said — that Fort Drum was going to be retained and Fort Ord was going to be closed. Fort Ord had twice demonstrated its suitability for deployment to Third

---

[557] Ibid.
[558] Ibid.
[559] Ibid.
[560] A. Emory (1992) "10th Mountain Division 'Double Halo' May be Drum's Savior," *Watertown Daily Times*, Dec. 15, p. 26.
[561] D.A. Rayno (1991) "Drum Opponent on Panel Helped Change it to Fort," *Watertown Daily Times*, June 8, p. 28.

World conflicts, once to Panama and once to the Persian Gulf.[562] Fort Drum has no such record and seems by all objective accounts unsuited for that type of mission.

The blatant inconsistencies of the Army's explanations for its requests came to a head when the topic turned from Fort Drum to Plattsburgh Air Force Base. Again, the base received a low ranking by objective cost-effectiveness measures. The Pentagon's argument that Plattsburgh was favored by good weather stood in sharp contrast to the careful avoidance of any mention of weather during the earlier Fort Drum discussions. The reporter for the *Watertown Daily Times* noted:

The weather argument drew repeated sarcastic reactions from commissioners, with Mr. Ball wondering wryly if they should consider weather as a determining factor in Army bases.[563]

But Fort Drum's weather was not discussed. The panel did acquiesce to Pentagon plans which were not made public. Fort Drum was spared, as eventually were Griffiss Air Force Base and Plattsburgh Air Force Base.[564] It is curious, if not worrisome, that three major military bases — without clear rationale — all in the same rural Congressional district bordering on central Canada, will stay operational for unspecified military plans and contingencies.

Later that year, Colonel (retired) David Hackworth, America's most decorated soldier, singled out Fort Drum as one Army base that should be closed if the real mission is rapid overseas deployment. [565] He called Fort Drum a "sacred cow."

---

[562] A. Emory (1991) "Fort Drum Escapes Ax: Panel Votes to Keep it, Despite Low Rating," *Watertown Daily Times*, June 8, p. 28.
[563] A. Emory (1991) "Air Force Ready to Fight to Save Plattsburgh, Loring, Griffiss," *Watertown Daily Times*, June 8, pp. 30, 28.
[564] Anon. (1991) "Commission Votes to Close 6 Big Air Force Installations," *New York Times*, June 29, p. 10.
[565] Colonel (retired) D.H. Hackworth (1991) "Amputation, Not Pedicure," *Newsweek*, Dec. 9, p. 35.
M. Smith (1991) "Vet, Author, Pentagon Critic Says Drum Should Be One of Bases Cut," *Watertown Daily Times*, Dec. 5.

CHAPTER 11

EXCUSES, RIDICULE AND RESPONSE

The concern that Fort Drum is now situated for military contingencies against Canada is based on facts, on the opinions of various experts and on reasonable inferences. Although there are thousands of guns at Fort Drum, no "smoking gun" has been found, no internal memo, no policy statement, no contingency plan, to conclusively prove the concerns valid. However, it is unlikely such would be left lying around. Former Deputy Undersecretary of the US Army, Thaddeus Holt, has written that the 1930s plans to attack Canada were, in their day, "among the most sensitive and closely held papers on earth."[566]

Concerns about US military preparations against Canada are inherently political in nature. Furthermore, the facts about Fort Drum are relatively unknown. For these reasons it has been relatively easy to find comments critical of concern that the US would prepare military forces for Canadian contingencies. Fortunately, there has been ample time and outlets for opinion and argument to be expressed. Since early 1990 when research on Fort

---

[566] T. Holt (1988) "Joint Plan Red," *MHQ: The Quarterly Journal of Military History*, vol. 1 (no. 1), p. 48.

Drum first appeared in the *Queen's Quarterly*,[567] the story has been reported by various newspapers and magazines, including the Kingston *Whig-Standard*,[568] the *Watertown Daily Times*,[569] the *Ottawa Citizen*,[570] the *Calgary Herald*,[571] *La Presse*,[572] the *Los Angeles Times*,[573] *Pravda*,[574] the Syracuse *Post-Standard*,[575] the New Zealand *Peacelink*,[576] the *Toronto Star*,[577] the *Canadian Geographic*,[578] the *Washington Post*[579] and the Manchester *Guardian Weekly*.[580] Many of these reports sought out and included expert opinion both supportive and critical of concern about Fort Drum. Many of these reports resulted in letters to the editor. These comments and criticisms will here be summarized, analyzed and responded to.

SUPPORT

The most consistent support for concern that Fort Drum might threaten Canada has come from professional historians. They know that the period of alliance and trust between Canada and the United States during World War II and the Cold War is but an episode, an

---

[567] F.W. Rudmin (1989) "Offensive Light Infantry Forces at Fort Drum, New York: Why Should Canadians Care?" *Queen's Quarterly*, vol. 96 (no. 4), pp. 886-917.

[568] D. Hogan (1990) "Too Close for Comfort? Military Experts Divided on Theory Fort Drum May be a Threat to Canada," *Whig-Standard*, March 24, p. 4.

[569] J. Golden (1990) "Professor Warns Drum Base for Ontario Strike," *Watertown Daily Times*, April 1, pp. B1,B6.
J. Golden (1990) "Invasion of Canada? He's Serious," *Watertown Daily Times*, April 8, pp. C1-C2.

[570] D. Pugliese (1990) "The Americans are Coming! The Americans are Coming!" *Ottawa Citizen*, Dec. 30, p. A1.

[571] D. Rowe (1990) "Theory Warns of US Invasion," *Calgary Herald*, Dec. 31, p. B6.

[572] Anon. (1990) "Le Canada est-il à l'abri d'une invasion armée des États-Unis?" *La Presse*, Dec. 31, p. A2.

[573] M.W. Walsh (1991) "Canadian Sees GIs Marching on Quebec," *Los Angeles Times*, Jan. 8, p. 2.

[574] V. Shelkov (1991) ["The Secrets of Fort Drum"], *Pravda*, Jan. 15.

[575] J.D. Salant (1991) "The War that Never Was," *Post-Standard*, March 25, pp. A1, A4.

[576] O. Wilkes (1991) "US may have Plans for Military Invasion of Canada," *Peacelink*, (no. 94), August, pp. 26-27.

[577] J. Picton (1991) "Is US Base Potential Threat to Canada?" *Toronto Star*, Dec. 1, p. A7.

[578] J. Sobol (1992) "Life Along the Line," *Canadian Geographic*, vol. 112 (no. 1), Jan.-Feb., pp. 46-56.

[579] W. Claiborne (1992) "Maple Leaf Rage: Canadians are Concerned over US Intentions should their Nation Break Up," *Washington Post*, March 1, p. C2.

[580] W. Claiborne (1992) "What will the US do if the Confederation Breaks Up?" *Guardian Weekly*, March 8, p. 17.

episode now finishing. Although that episode encompasses most contemporary living memory, it is not representative of other periods of history. It is not a reliable basis on which to judge future US strategic planning. Much of the public and even highly placed military authorities, however, tend to misperceive history based on this recent episode of alliance. They use that misperception as a basis for confidence in predicting future US military intentions. For example, Major Don Marsh, spokesman for Canada's Defence Minister, discounted concern about Fort Drum because Canadian relations with the United States "have always been good."[581] US Brigadier-General Charles McClain, Chief of Public Affairs, cites the same misperception:

> Whatever the future may bring, the 10th Mountain Division will be ready for a variety of challenges, and the United States and Canada will continue to stand together — the strong friends they have been for two centuries.[582]

This is in contrast to the two anonymous reviewers recommending publication of the initial Fort Drum research in the *Queen's Quarterly*. Both were, it turned out, historians. Said one:

> If the Canadians know the real purpose of Drum, either through intelligence work or through an accident, no one holding any position of authority or responsibility would comment on it for obvious reasons. Nor would the American military do so, again for obvious reasons ... Three points stand out ... The Americans will act in their own interest whatever they perceive it to be, and they may well be more dangerous to neighbors as the Soviet menace recedes. They cannot live without a cause. The second point is that there is plenty of room for speculation about the *raison d'être* of the base just from a consideration of the uses to which it seems to be put ... The third point is the historical one that shows the traditional rivalries, in the area, between the two countries. This is strong and provides the real reason for publishing the paper. There is a powerful historical consistency in the attitudes on both sides of the border.

Said the other historian:

> I recommend that you publish it as is. The author has made a good argument, the matter should be discussed, and it is important that Canadians remember

---

[581] D. Pugliese (1991) "Invasion 1930: US had Plan to Attack Canada to Win Economic Battle with Britain," *Ottawa Citizen*, March 27, pp. A1-A2.
[582] Brigadier-General C.W. McClain, Jr. (1991) "Ft. Drum and Canada" (letter), *Los Angeles Times*, Jan. 24, p. 6.

that the United States is, if not *just* another foreign country, a foreign country with interests that are not necessarily either our own or in our own interests.

Donald Schurman, a retired professor of military history at Canada's Royal Military College, said that many people would be outraged by this analysis, but he himself is not.[583] He later added, "I thought it was good that Rudmin wrote his paper because people who say there are no contingency plans [for Canada] don't know military or foreign affairs."[584] Gabriel Kolko, Distinguished Professor of Research at York University and a specialist on diplomatic history, made a similar argument: "I think you must know that the US has contingency plans for every situation, and I've worked in this area for 30 years now."[585] Christopher Cushing, with the Canadian Institute of Strategic Studies, said "It would be imprudent of the Pentagon not to have a plan. They have people whose job is to think of every possible contingency whether it is for 1930 or now."[586] He noted that the plan to move troops to the Persian Gulf was formulated three years in advance.[587]

Support has also been expressed by several people who study covert US foreign policy. For example, Noam Chomsky, the Massachusetts Institute of Technology linguistics professor who writes and speaks widely on US foreign policy, said to a *Toronto Star* reporter:

I have no special knowledge, but Rudmin's arguments seem to me to be very plausible and worth serious attention. He is not a crackpot. I have studied US planning world-wide, and there's nothing out of line [with his hypothesis].[588]

To the same reporter, Louis Wolfe, editor of the Washington-based *Covert Action Information Bulletin*, said:

---

[583] D. Hogan (1990) "Too Close for Comfort? Military Experts Divided on Theory Fort Drum May be a Threat to Canada," *Whig-Standard*, March 24, p. 4.
[584] J. Picton (1991) "Is US Base Potential Threat to Canada?" *Toronto Star*, Dec. 1, p. A7.
[585] Ibid.
[586] D. Pugliese (1991) "Invasion 1930: US had Plan to Attack Canada to Win Economic Battle with Britain," *Ottawa Citizen*, March 27, pp. A1-A2.
[587] P. Peirol (1991) "US Plan to Attack Canada in 1930 Causes Stir," *Whig-Standard*, March 27, p. 2.

Frankly, I think there is some merit to Rudmin's theory. The responses, I found, to his papers and some of the justifications [for Drum] offered by the administration were ridiculous ... The commander of that region said the troops were for deployment in South America, but they get more snow there [in the Fort Drum region] than almost any part of the country — and that is very questionable.[589]

Finally, many people within the peace community have endorsed concern about Fort Drum. The president of Science for Peace, David Parnas, is a computer scientist most noted for his resignation from a chief consultancy position in the "Star Wars" project to become one of its most severe and successful critics. In the past, he had had employment with various US defence contractors and agencies, including the CIA. Professor Parnas wrote:

As someone who has worked within the US military establishment for many years, I am certain of a few things: (1) the US military believes in planning for every contingency that they can think of, (2) the US military believes that Canada is important to the defence of the US, (3) the US has seriously considered the basing of "Star Wars" equipment on Canadian territory, (4) if, as is often stated, Panama and the other Central American countries are the US's backyard, Canada is its front porch, (5) the US has no hesitation about using its armed forces when it believes that its interests are threatened.

No Canadian is in a position to know what plans the US has, and Prof. Rudmin was careful not to claim that he knew. Those who responded to his well researched and well documented article did not report errors in fact or successfully refute his logic. All that they could do was poke fun at the idea.[590]

Owen Wilkes, editor of the New Zealand *Peacelink* magazine, also thought that concern about Fort Drum was plausible and prudent.[591] Ernie Regehr, coordinator of Project Ploughshares, agreed that Fort Drum is a potential intervention force but argued that Canada's best defence is to prevent conditions of internal disorder that might justify US military intervention.[592] John McMurtry, professor of philosophy at the University of Guelph, has also agreed that Fort

---

[588] J. Picton (1991) "Is US Base Potential Threat to Canada?" *Toronto Star*, Dec. 1, p. A7.
[589] Ibid.
[590] D.L. Parnas (1990) "Fort Drum Scoffers Can't Cite Factual Errors" (letter), *Whig-Standard*, April 26, p. 7.
[591] O. Wilkes (1991) "US may have Plans for Military Invasion of Canada," *Peacelink*, (no. 94), August, pp. 26-27.
[592] E. Regehr (1990) "Should Canadians Worry about Fort Drum?," *Toronto Star*, May 3, p. A29.

Drum threatens Canada.[593] He has directed particular criticism at the Canadian defence establishment for acquiescing to a hostile US military posture.[594]

FAINT PRAISE

Another kind of support has come from several strategic planning experts who have praised the research leading to the conclusion that Fort Drum threatens Canada, but who have explicitly rejected that conclusion. Foremost of these is Les Aspin, former Chairman of the House Armed Services Committee, sometime critic of US interventionist policies and now Secretary of Defense for the Clinton administration. After reading a draft of the initial research on Fort Drum, Aspin wrote:

I appreciate you sending me your paper on Ft. Drum. It is a masterful piece of research. Knowing what I know of the US military planning process and US government decision-making, I cannot agree with your conclusion, however.

You are correct that attitudes can change and one cannot rule out the theoretical possibility of an eventual Canadian-American confrontation. However, that is so far down the "threat" scale that it is not a consideration for the placement of one of only 21 US (Army and Marine Corps) divisions.

More importantly, let me note that contiguity is not a key in US military planning as implied in your analysis. Deployment of forces on an intercontinental scale is restricted by distance, but not deployment of force on an intra-continental scale. Let me note that units deployed to invade Grenada came from as far as the State of Washington. Abolishing Fort Drum would not have one iota of impact on any "decision" to invade Canada. The capability existed long before the 10th Mountain Division was placed at Fort Drum and would still exist should Fort Drum be dis-established.[595]

This response by Aspin has created some old-style Cold War furor. On March 20, 1991, a Mr. Jeff Moore of the US Information Agency called to inform me that the January 15, 1991, issue of

---

[593] J. McMurtry (1990) "Canada Must Wake up to US Threat" (letter), *Toronto Star*, May 10, p. A26.

[594] J. McMurtry (1992) "Expensive Weakling" (letter), *Globe and Mail*, March 11, p. A15.

[595] L. Aspin (1989) Personal letter, March 7.

Pravda had carried a report of my analysis of Fort Drum.[596] The report included Aspin's statement about "masterful piece of research." The Agency suspected that *Pravda* had fabricated the Aspin quotation as part of a campaign of disinformation intended to slander the United States. Mr. Moore faxed me a copy and a translation of the report. It was competent, certainly comparable to North American journalism. In fact, the quotation in question must have been copied from the *Ottawa Citizen*. [597] *Pravda*'s writing was prosaic, free of provocative rhetoric or overstatements. It even explained that most people would find the idea of a US attack on Canada difficult to accept.

Faint praise, similar to Aspin's, has also come from Major-General (retired) Leonard Johnson, former Commandant of Canada's National Defence College and now director of Project Ploughshares. Like Aspin, Johnson represents military expertise that is nevertheless critical of militarism. He told the Kingston *Whig-Standard* that the research on Fort Drum "was very thorough."[598] But he added that it reads "like damn good fiction," probably referring to the novels about a US attack on Canada written by his colleague Major-General (retired) Richard Rohner.[599] Johnson explained that he presumes that Fort Drum was probably chosen because of available space. Which, it should be added, is not correct since one of the reasons the base was recommended for closure is because it is overcrowded.[600] Said Johnson, "I don't believe that they are likely to take military action against Canada. They can get

[596] V. Shelkov (1991) ["The Secrets of Fort Drum"], *Pravda*, Jan. 15.

[597] D. Pugliese (1990) "The Americans are Coming! The Americans are Coming!" *Ottawa Citizen*, Dec. 30, p. A1.

[598] D. Hogan (1990) "Too Close for Comfort? Military Experts Divided on Theory Fort Drum May be a Threat to Canada," *Whig-Standard*, March 24, p. 4.

[599] R. Rohner (1973) *Ultimatum*, Vancouver: Clarke, Irwin.

   R. Rohner (1974) *Exoneration*, Toronto: McClelland and Stuart.

[600] A. Emory (1991) "Fort Drum Escapes Ax: Panel Votes to Keep it, Despite Low Rating," *Watertown Daily Times*, June 8, pp. 30, 26.

enough here through the boardroom and the checkbook."[601] Like Aspin, Johnson also argued that the United States would not need a light infantry division at Fort Drum in order to seize Ottawa since it has airborne divisions that have been quite capable of doing that all along.[602]

A third instance of complimenting the research but rejecting the conclusion has come from Alex Morrison, director of the Canadian Institute of Strategic Studies. He told the *Ottawa Citizen* that "Rudmin builds a convincing argument," but that "there's really no reason for the US to invade Canada because they already own half of it." [603]

Finally, Captain Rick Jones, spokesman for the Canadian Department of National Defence, said of the *Queen's Quarterly* article, "Our position is it's an apparently well-researched document." He declined to speak for or against the conclusion but did affirm faith in US goodwill based on World War II alliance: "Canada and the US were staunch allies. We consider ourselves to be reliable partners in defence. That's proven in the past."[604] In fact, a full and accurate account of the past proves the contrary.

Two years later, the executive assistant to the Canadian Chief of Defence Staff sent an unsolicited letter to the *Watertown Daily Times* dismissing any concern that Fort Drum might threaten Canadian security and independence:

I would like to assure you that neither the Department of Defence nor the Canadian Forces places any credence in such a suggestion.[605]

Déjà vu 1935.

---

[601] D. Hogan (1990) "Too Close for Comfort? Military Experts Divided on Theory Fort Drum May be a Threat to Canada," *Whig-Standard*, March 24, p. 4.

[602] Major-General (retired) L. Johnson (1987) Personal communication, Oct. 22.

[603] D. Pugliese (1990) "The Americans are Coming! The Americans are Coming!" *Ottawa Citizen*, Dec. 30, p. A1.

[604] D. Hogan (1990) "Too Close for Comfort? Military Experts Divided on Theory Fort Drum May be a Threat to Canada," *Whig-Standard*, March 24, p. 4.

[605] M. Smith (1992) "Canada Shrugs Off Theory of Threat by US," *Watertown Daily Times*, April 26, pp. A1, A9.

It is not common for research to be complimented while the inference drawn from that research is rejected. The reason for rejecting concern about US capabilities and intentions is, in essence: "The United States has other means of military and economic control of Canada and does not need to have assault forces at Fort Drum for Canadian contingencies. Therefore, those forces do not threaten Canada." There are several responses to this type of reasoning. First, rather than mitigating military threat to Canada, extensive US interests and ownership in Canada would more likely aggravate and justify US readiness to intrude. That is the usual interpretation of "interests" and it has been well articulated in reference to Canada in US strategic planning circles.[606] Second, as the history of US military preparations shows, the United States is more aggressive just when economic ties are tightening. Canada had negotiated free trade agreements with the United States during the Taft administration in the early years of this century and during the Roosevelt administration in the 1930s. Those were the very periods of most intensive secret US military preparations for war on Canada. In the 1980s and 90s, Canada-US economic integration is being implemented, going further and faster than any of those earlier attempts. US military contingency preparations would presumably keep pace.

Finally, given a presumption of hostility and knowledge of long-range attack capabilities, then one should be more, not less, concerned about new rapid attack capabilities near at hand. Aspin's and Johnson's reasoning is not persuasive and certainly not reassuring. Their argument is reminiscent of the 1935 dismissal of concern about the border air base since US capability to bomb Canada would exist with or without the base. But the historical fact is that US military planners nevertheless did seek a border base for the explicit purpose of rapid attack on Canada. Aspin's and

---

[606] D.E. Nuechterlein (1985) "North America: Our Neglected Heartland," *Parameters: Journal of the US Army War College*, vol. 15 (no. 3), pp. 58-65.

Johnson's argument is like saying that the United States should not have been concerned about Soviet nuclear missiles in Cuba in the 1960s because the Soviets could have started a nuclear war with or without missiles there. Their reasoning also needs to confront the fact that the United States has long had other units quite capable of performing any of the conceivable missions of Fort Drum's light infantry. Military journals are full of statements that existing airborne and Marine divisions, as well as Ranger and Special Forces units, could already do anything that light infantry divisions might be called upon to do. Yet, the light divisions were created nevertheless. The major advantages of light infantry are their fast deployment — at least locally — and their specialization in urban combat against civilian forces. For fast, effective and limited deployment into Ottawa or Montreal, there is no substitute for a light division at Fort Drum. Also, a military intrusion from a local base would seem more "neighbourly," helpful, and unplanned, less like a premeditated hostile invasion.

EXCUSES

Several critics have tried to argue that Fort Drum has perfectly plausible missions for which it is well-situated. Hence, they argue that there is no need to invent or imagine a covert Canadian mission. For example, Canadian Brigadier-General (retired) Donald Macnamara has said that the "obvious reason" that a light division was based at Fort Drum was "because there are few cold-weather training environments in the United States."[607] The Honourable Perrin Beatty, Minister of National Defence in 1988, expressed much the same opinion.[608] In response, it should be noted that cold-weather training may explain the need for a training base at Fort Drum, but not the permanent garrisoning of an assault division

---

[607] D. Hogan (1990) "Too Close for Comfort? Military Experts Divided on Theory Fort Drum May be a Threat to Canada," Whig-Standard, March 24, p. 4,
[608] P. Beatty (1988) Personal letter, January 7.

there. During the 1991 hearings of the Base Closure and Realignment Commission, one argument for retaining Fort Drum was that it was a "fighting" installation, not a "training" base.[609]

Macnamara has further argued that Fort Drum's 10th Division might be destined to defend NATO's northern flank in Norway, to replace Canada's withdrawn Nordic brigade.[610] However, Michael Ganley, criticizing Fort Drum in the *Armed Forces Journal International*, had clearly anticipated Macnamara's supposition and dismissed it: "Marine Corps units are assigned principal responsibility for reinforcing NATO's northern flank, and equipment for them is now being prepositioned there."[611] Furthermore, the head of the Army's European Command, General Howard Stone, gave testimony to Congress in 1984 that he was not consulted about the new Fort Drum forces and doubts their usefulness in the European theatre.[612] They have little anti-armour capability and only a 48-hour supply infrastructure.

US Senator Alfonse D'Amato, Republican, from New York State, is a member of the Senate Intelligence Committee and the Appropriations Committee's defense sub-committee. He is also one of the principle lobbyists for Fort Drum. When pressed by the Syracuse *Post-Standard* to state where Fort Drum's forces might be used, Senator D'Amato answered, "What about rapid deployment in Eastern Europe?"[613] He had to guess. A man in his position apparently did not know where Fort Drum forces might be used. It seems that, officially, no one does. D'Amato, too, seems ignorant

[609] A. Emory (1991) "Fort Drum Escapes Ax: Panel Votes to Keep it, Despite Low Rating," *Watertown Daily Times*, June 8, pp. 30, 26.
[610] D. Hogan (1990) "Too Close for Comfort? Military Experts Divided on Theory Fort Drum May be a Threat to Canada," *Whig-Standard*, March 24, p. 4,
    D. Gore (1988) "Canada Needs to Bolster World Military Role: Brig. General," *Queen's Journal*, Sept. 30, p. 3.
[611] M. Ganley (1985) "Are Soldiers Headed for 'Hot' Spots Doomed to Train at Frigid Fort Drum?" *Armed Forces Journal International*, vol. 122 (no. 10), p. 78.
[612] M.R. Gordon (1985) "Army's Third World Strike Force Finds a Home — in Alaska of All Cold Places," *National Journal*, vol. 7, April 14, p. 728.
[613] J.D. Salant (1991) "The War that Never Was;" *Post-Standard* (Syracuse), March 25, p. A4.

of the testimony of the Army's European commander. And even if light infantry were useful in Europe, Fort Drum does not have an airfield suitable for overseas deployment. And even if it did, says an Army report, Fort Drum's bad weather would hamper deployment.[614] Wrote Major Louis D. Huddleston in *Military Review*:

> The light infantry division was not intended to fight in Europe ... The chances of US fighting forces becoming involved in armed conflict in Europe are remote. The United States has vital interests in other places around the world, and these are much more likely to be threatened. A suitable battlefield awaits the light infantry division, but it is not a European setting.[615]

Nevertheless, US Army Lieutenant-Colonel Adolf Carlson has argued that Fort Drum forces are suited for rapid deployment to Europe. He said that in the event of a general land war in Europe, and in the event that the United States would have to ship troops by boat from southern US ports, and in the event that Cuba would intercept those ships, then Fort Drum's forces are perfectly situated to fly to the rescue of NATO and save the day.[616] He, too, is evidently unaware of the European Command's doubt about the utility of light infantry and unaware of the difficulties of rapid air deployment from Fort Drum.

Lieutenant-Colonel Carlson is also the only one to challenge any of facts of evidence presented in the original *Queen's Quarterly* article. In that article, I wrote, "It is widely acknowledged that the 6th Division [in Alaska] is not really intended for overseas deployment."[617] The point was that not all light infantry are destined for missions outside North America. Lieutenant-Colonel Carlson, in a letter to the Kingston *Whig-Standard*, wrote:

---

[614] M. Ganley (1985) "Are Soldiers Headed for 'Hot' Spots Doomed to Train at Frigid Fort Drum?" *Armed Forces Journal International*, vol. 122 (no. 10), p. 84.
[615] Major L.D. Huddleston (1985) "Light Infantry Division: Azimuth Check," *Military Review*, vol. 65 (no. 9), p. 16.
[616] Lieutenant-Colonel A. Carlson (1990) "Strategic for Deployment" (letter), *Whig-Standard*, April 26, p. 7.
[617] F.W. Rudmin (1989) "Offensive Light Infantry Forces at Fort Drum, New York: Why Should Canadians Care?" *Queen's Quarterly*, vol. 96 (no. 4), p. 895.

By the way, Prof. Rudmin's contention that the 6th Infantry Division is not intended for overseas deployment is incorrect. Even in peacetime, the 6th Division is assigned to the headquarters charged with the defence of Korea.[618]

There is no reason to doubt Carlson's information about the command structure for the 6th Division. However, the fact remains that the US Army has stated that the "primary mission" of the 6th Light Infantry Division is "the defense of Alaska."[619] Army spokesman Lieutenant-Colonel Craig MacNab has said that "the 6th Division will be keyed on Alaska itself."[620] Michael Gordon, writing in the *National Journal*, brought forward logistic evidence that the 6th Division is not destined for overseas deployment:

The new 6th Division is also to be equipped with special winter boots, winter camouflage and other Arctic equipment that will make it somewhat heavier than other light divisions and therefore more difficult to transport. It will also have fewer wheeled vehicles and trucks than other divisions. Instead, most of its vehicles will have tracks that allow them to operate in snow. Because the Army does not expect to deploy the division to a foreign trouble spot, it has not conducted an analysis of how many aircraft sorties it would take to transport the division.[621]

A more common defence of Fort Drum accepts the premise that it makes little military sense to base a rapid deployment assault division at Fort Drum, but argues that it is just a mistake, just a bungle, entailing no covert contingency plans for Canada. Therefore, Canadians should not be concerned about Fort Drum.

For example, Canadian Lieutenant-Colonel Rick Williams, one of five principal staff officers at Canadian Forces Base Kingston, said that it is illogical to presume that because there is no other conceivable reason to put assault troops at Fort Drum that they

---

[618] Lieutenant-Colonel A. Carlson (1990) "Strategic for Deployment" (letter), *Whig-Standard*, April 26, p. 7.

[619] S.D. Goose (1988) "Low-Intensity Warfare: The Warriors and their Weapons," in M. Klare and P. Kornbluh (eds.), *Low-Intensity Warfare* (pp. 80-111), New York: Pantheon Books, p. 101.

[620] M.R. Gordon (1985) "Army's Third World Strike Force Finds a Home — in Alaska of All Cold Places," *National Journal*, vol. 7, April 14, p. 731.

[621] Ibid., p. 729.

must be there to threaten Canada.[622] Rear-Admiral (retired) Eugene Carroll made almost the same argument:

Drum survived a lot of pressure to close it. New York has a lot of members of Congress and they didn't want to see it closed. There are more than 100 US bases due to close by 1997 to save money. He [Rudmin] is taking the fact that since [Drum] is not a suitable site [for the 10th Mountain], he's inferring that it has evil intentions.[623]

It is realistic, not illogical, to look at a military base's capabilities to surmise its use. It is best to make no presumptions about intentions or motivations. It is the critics who here wish to do so, to dismiss any discussion of capabilities on the false presumption that the United States has always been, is now and ever will be a trustworthy and forthright friend of Canada.

Other critics have voiced Rear-Admiral Carroll's claim that Fort Drum is just the result of political patronage. For example, Brigadier-General (retired) Donald Macnamara said that northern New York may have been "owed a favor somewhere in the system."[624] David Sokolsky, professor at Canada's Royal Military College, said, "There's no factual evidence to support the view that the base is there for any reason other than political patronage."[625] As argued earlier, political patronage and pork-barrelling are difficult to rule out since they seem to influence almost all government spending. But their universality also means that they do not explain decisions nor give reasons for presuming that politically influenced decisions are benign. Would the Soviet Union have been less concerned about Trident nuclear submarines if they had known that the construction contracts were influenced by patronage?

---

[622] D. Hogan (1990) "Too Close for Comfort? Military Experts Divided on Theory Fort Drum May be a Threat to Canada," *Whig-Standard*, March 24, p. 4.
[623] J. Picton (1991) "Is US Base Potential Threat to Canada?" *Toronto Star*, Dec. 1, p. A7.
[624] D. Hogan (1990) "Too Close for Comfort? Military Experts Divided on Theory Fort Drum May be a Threat to Canada," *Whig-Standard*, March 24, p. 4.
[625] J. Picton (1991) "Is US Base Potential Threat to Canada?" *Toronto Star*, Dec. 1, p. A7.

As would be expected in any military project of the scale of Fort Drum, there has been misuse and diversion of public funds. The question is, why would the Army, at the very highest levels of command, knowingly cooperate in this? One answer is that it wants an expanded base at Fort Drum at any cost and will do anything to maintain the well-orchestrated local political lobby. The waste of tens of millions of dollars for Fort Drum's water is one documented example of fraud and corruption at the base.

In 1989, a top civil servant at the base explained why there was no need to pipe water to the base from the Black River:

Beneath Fort Drum is a massive aquifer filled with water of 'exceptionally high quality' and of quantities more than enough to meet the highest projected needs of the expanded post. [626]

Hydrologists from the US Geological Survey and from the Army Corps of Engineers had independently mapped and certified this water supply.[627] It was public knowledge:

Development of wells tapped into the massive aquifer beneath Fort Drum would cost "substantially less" than the construction of a proposed Fort Drum-to-Watertown fresh water pipeline. [628]

The base's existing deep wells, seventeen in number, were more than adequate to meet peak demands, with excess capacity to spare.

Nevertheless, US Army Secretary John O. Marsh personally authorized an illegal, noncompetitive contract to pipe water twelve miles uphill from the Black River.[629] The pipeline cost $16,000,000

---

[626] M.J. Davis (1989) "Wells Sufficient for Fort: Drum Doesn't Need to Spend Money on Pipeline," *Watertown Daily Times*, Mar. 2, pp. 26, 22.

[627] Ibid.

D. Jenkins (1988) "Drum has Water" (letter),*Watertown Daily Times*, Dec. 29.

[628] M.J. Davis (1989) "Drum's Own Wells Cheaper than Line," *Watertown Daily Times*, Mar. 2, pp. 30, 22, quoting from p. 22.

[629] D. Jenkins (1991) (untitled letter), *Carthage Republican Tribune*, Nov. 13.

to build.[630] The supplier buys river water from the City of Watertown at less than one dollar per thousand gallons, mixes it with free base well water, and sells the concoction to the Army at six dollars per thousand gallons.[631] Internal Army memoranda reveal that the Army knew it had ample water supplies on base, knew that noncompetitive procurement was unjustified, and was concerned to avoid "additional Congressional scrutiny of Fort Drum."[632] The question is, why?

The retention of Fort Drum by the Base Closure and Realignment Commission in June, 1991, further shows that it is the Pentagon that wants a base at Fort Drum, at any cost. The evidence is that the Commission was not responsive to political pressures. Senator Kennedy could not save Fort Devon in Massachusetts. The Senate Majority Leader, George Mitchell, could not save Loring Air Force Base in Maine. Mitchell is one of the most powerful politicians in Washington. Rear-Admiral (retired) Eugene Carroll, referring to "intense political pressures" on the Commission, said that "Maine has the strongest possible makeup in the Senate."[633] These powerful senators could not save their bases but critics would like to argue that a relatively low-ranking Congressman could muster the political clout to save three major military bases — Fort Drum, Griffiss Air Force Base, Plattsburgh Air Force Base — all in the same rural riding. It is not believable.

A related excuse is that Fort Drum was expanded for reasons of regional economic development. For example, Terrence Roche, former commander at Fort Drum, has said that the base was built to inject government money into a sagging local economy: "To me

---

[630] M.J. Davis (1989) "Drum's Own Wells Cheaper than Line," *Watertown Daily Times*, Mar. 2, pp. 30, 22, quoting from p. 22.
[631] D. Jenkins (1991) (untitled letter), *Carthage Republican Tribune*, Nov. 13.
[632] Ibid.
[633] J. Mathewson (1991) "PAFB on Base-Closing 'Short List,'" *Press-Republican* (Plattsburgh, NY), June 8, pp. 1, 13, quoting from p. 13.

the bottom line was to help an area that economically needed it."[634] Canadian military analyst Alex Morrison has articulated the same excuse: "While Fort Drum may be a questionable military location for the 10th Division, it isn't unusual for the US government to use defence spending to boost a region's economy."[635] Brigadier-General (retired) Donald Macnamara has said, "Regional development probably also played an important role in choosing the site of northern New York."[636]

As with patronage, it should be noted, local economic benefits always arise from all US military spending. It is universal, and therefore relatively uninformative. In any case, as discussed in Chapter 3, other states and other counties seeking the 10th Division garrison had far greater economic need than did northern New York. Furthermore, the Base Closure and Realignment Commission did not consider economic needs when it retained Fort Drum.

Other comments and explanations by military authorities concerning Fort Drum seem equally unpersuasive. For example, knowledge of the existence of actual US plans to attack Canada should shake confidence that the United States would never make such plans. However, some strategic specialists see no problem with that. Major-General (retired) Ernie Creber has said that both US and Canadian military officials continually make plans for various scenarios. "But they have no meaning unless there are political orders to go ahead with such schemes."[637] Yet, the whole thrust of concern about Fort Drum is that it appears that the US military is actually going ahead with preparations. Furthermore, military analysts have warned that the need to use light infantry in

---

[634] D. Pugliese (1990) "The Americans are Coming! The Americans are Coming!" *Ottawa Citizen*, Dec. 30, p. A1.
[635] Ibid.
[636] D. Hogan (1990) "Too Close for Comfort? Military Experts Divided on Theory Fort Drum May be a Threat to Canada," *Whig-Standard*, March 24, p. 4.
[637] D. Pugliese (1991) "Invasion 1930: US had Plan to Attack Canada to Win Economic Battle with Britain," *Ottawa Citizen*, March 27, pp. A1-A2.

haste may lead to their use in anticipation of political consultation and consensus.

One unique argument was made by Lawrence Korb, a former US Assistant Secretary of Defense and currently a member of the Brookings Institution in Washington, D.C. He was in the Pentagon when Fort Drum was chosen for expansion. He seems to agree that the base is less than ideal for rapid deployment light infantry but insists that Fort Drum has nothing to do with Canada, that the site was chosen because it was the most economical alternative, especially considering New York State's contribution to roads and housing.[638] In other words, Fort Drum was a good buy. However, that seems inconsistent with the fact that a 1983 Army study estimated that the Fort Drum alternative would be the most expensive, by $200,000,000, and with the fact that Lieutenant-Colonel Joseph Terry, head of the Army's Light Division Command, went on record in 1985 saying that "the Fort Drum alternative is the most expensive."[639] *The Washington Post's* 1985 account of the basing decision, which was circulated by Congressman Martin's office, states:

Fort Drum was chosen as home of the new 10th Mountain Division, despite Army projections of higher development costs there than at competing military installations in Alaska, Washington state, Kentucky, Georgia and California.[640]

There is also the fact that the Army Auditing Agency in 1991 ranked Fort Drum worst of all Army bases under consideration for closure by the Base Closure and Realignment Commission.[641] Thus, economics does not seem a viable explanation for putting an assault division on the Canadian border.

---

[638] J. Picton (1991) "Is US Base Potential Threat to Canada?" *Toronto Star*, Dec. 1, p. A7.

[639] M. Ganley (1985) "Are Soldiers Headed for 'Hot' Spots Doomed to Train at Frigid Fort Drum?" *Armed Forces Journal International*, vol. 122 (no. 10), p. 80.

[640] M. Weisskopf (1985) "Community Happily Anticipates Army Invasion," *Washington Post*, May 27, p. A3.

[641] A. Emory (1991) "Fort Drum Escapes Ax: Panel Votes to Keep it, Despite Low Rating," *Watertown Daily Times*, June 8, pp. 30, 28.

Thomas Durell Young, a research professor at the US Army War College's Strategic Studies Institute, said that the United States would not attack Canada because we all share a common Anglo-Saxon heritage. This comment is published right under a map showing US invasion routes into Ontario and Quebec. *War Plan Red*, which Professor Young apparently had not seen, explicitly states:

> ... despite racial affinity, common culture and similar political systems ... it is believed that the BLUE [US] government would experience little difficulty in mobilizing public sentiment in favor of a vigorous prosecution of the war, once hostilities began. [642]

The plan even called for the aggressive use of poison gas against Canadians. Clearly, Anglo-Saxon solidarity is not much of a defence.

Another less than encouraging argument by Canadian military authorities is that no concern should be given to US military preparations against Canada since long alliance and integrated command place Canadian defence capabilities within Pentagon care. For example, Alex Morrison, director of the Canadian Institute for Strategic Studies, said that there is no need for concern about US military preparations against Canada because "the two countries have had close military ties since the signing of a joint US-Canada defence agreement 50 years ago."[643] Brigadier-General (retired) Lloyd Skaalan, who was once in charge of Canada-US defence planning, said "that ties between the military of both countries are now so close the existence of any modern invasion plans would be known."[644] Brigadier-General (retired) Donald Macnamara has said that he personally knows US military planners and none of them ever told him about contingency plans against

---

[642] *War Plan Red*, p. 38.

[643] D. Pugliese (1990) "The Americans are Coming! The Americans are Coming!" *Ottawa Citizen*, Dec. 30, p. A1.

[644] D. Pugliese (1991) "Invasion 1930: US had Plan to Attack Canada to Win Economic Battle with Britain," *Ottawa Citizen*, March 27, pp. A1-A2.

Canada:[645] "There never was an inkling of the existence of invasion plans for Canada."[646] This kind of thinking is supposed to give Canadians confidence? It seems to prove correct A.R.M. Lower's concerns in 1946 about the consequences of integrating Canadian defence into Pentagon command. He said:

If Canada wishes to become a subordinate state and even a more complete satellite of the United States than she is at present, the surest road for her to take is to accept American assistance to defending her own territories.[647]

RIDICULE

Those who wish to oppose the idea that Fort Drum might threaten Canada, but who have nothing substantive to say, typically turn to ridicule. As was discussed in the chapter on "Manifest Destiny," ridicule has historically been the technique favored to dismiss concern that the United States might have designs on Canada. Ridicule serves several purposes. On the surface, it appears to be a claim that the target of the ridicule is not worthy of a serious response. If that truly were the case, however, there would be no response. In fact, ridicule typically carries an angry, anxious, emotional tone. Ridiculers feel compelled to respond but are not able to say something serious. Ridicule allows them to simultaneously vent emotions, retain their own self-regard and undermine that of their target, all the while ignoring the issues.

Much of the written public reaction to the idea that the United States might prepare military contingencies against Canada has been ridicule, often with mention of other anxieties. Some examples:

---

[645] D. Gore (1988) "Canada Needs to Bolster World Military Role: Brig. General," *Queen's Journal*, Sept. 30, p. 3.
[646] D. Pugliese (1990) "The Americans are Coming! The Americans are Coming!" *Ottawa Citizen*, Dec. 30, p. A1.
[647] P. Resnick (1970) "Canadian Defence Policy and the American Empire," in I. Lumsden (ed.), *Close the 49th Parallel Etc.: The Americanization of Canada* (pp. 93-115), Toronto: University of Toronto Press, p. 99.

How amusing that, as the Warsaw Pact dissolves in confusion, our campus communists and their silly dupes, finding themselves in dire distress, feebly counterattack by inventing an American threat.[648]

It is not a preposterous idea that the US should want Canada, they just can't afford to take over Canada. We would set a bad example for the American public, for they would want the same social benefits that we have, costing the US government many billions of dollars they can't afford.[649]

And if Prof. Rudmin's research accomplishes nothing else, it will help divert our minds from the takeover of our beloved country by Quebec.[650]

Prof. Rudmin does an admirable job of aping the super-patriotic hypernationalists who would try to convince us that the enemies of Canada lie under every rock, tree, and Bush. But these people deserve more than just our derision: they could conceivably constitute a serious threat to the open nature of Canadian public life, leading the way to feminist-style witch-hunts ... [651]

The 10,000 troops at Fort Drum are there to defend the Americans against the encroaching hordes of Canadian shoppers invading all the border US shopping malls.[652]

Such ridicule was not unexpected. I myself wrote that "people on both sides of the border would find this a laughable scenario."[653] US political critic, Noam Chomsky, also had forewarned that ridicule would be the probable response but said that that is not his reaction: "On the contrary, it seems eminently realistic to suppose that intimidation might become an element of US policy."[654] David Parnas thought such ridicule was a nervous response to something "too frightening to really think about."[655]

One type of argument that comes frequently from military men is the exaggerated analogy. This has appeared surprisingly often in criticisms of the idea that Fort Drum might threaten Canada. The

---

[648] C. de L. Kirby (1990) "A Chuckle over Fort Drum" (letter), *Whig-Standard*, April 3, p. 4.

[649] N.J. Williamson (1990) "US couldn't Afford us" (letter), *Whig-Standard*, April 3, p. 4.

[650] A. Duffie (1990) "Oiling the Muskets against Fort Drum Threat" (letter), *Whig-Standard*, April 14, p. 8.

[651] T.J. Radcliffe (1990) "Every Rock, Tree, Bush" (letter), *Whig-Standard*, April 14, p. 8.

[652] D.O. McLean (1991) "Drum Beats" (letter), *Ottawa Citizen*, Jan. 10, p. A12.

[653] F.W. Rudmin (1989) "Offensive Light Infantry Forces at Fort Drum, New York: Why Should Canadians Care?" *Queen's Quarterly*, vol. 96 (no. 4), p. 902.

[654] N. Chomsky (1988) Personal letter, November 17.

[655] D.L. Parnas (1990) "Fort Drum Scoffers Can't Cite Factual Errors" (letter), *Whig-Standard*, April 26, p. 7.

technique is to present an extreme analogy that typically disparages the possibility of the US having any motives for military actions against Canada. These analogies sometimes reveal underlying beliefs.

An example of exaggerated analogy for satiric effect comes from Brigadier-General (retired) Donald Macnamara.[656] When asked about Fort Drum during a public lecture on Canadian defence, he responded that to say that Fort Drum threatens Ottawa is like saying that US strategic nuclear missiles in North Dakota are aimed at Vancouver. In both cases there are US military forces on the Canadian border and because it is absurd for the US to destroy Vancouver by nuclear missiles, it is by analogy absurd for the US to occupy Ottawa or Montreal by light infantry.

When the Syracuse *Post-Standard* reported on *War Plan Red*, it sought out the response of New York's Senator Alfonse D'Amato. He said:

If it is suggested you build Fort Drum to invade Canada, therefore he [Rudmin] should be able to draw the natural conclusion that those of us in New York who champion the cause of the Staten Island homeport did so with the ultimate design to conquer and invade New Jersey.[657]

In his mind, obviously, Canada is already the property of the United States. Also, he neglects the fact that the New York naval base has plausible missions other than attacking New Jersey.

Rear-Admiral (retired) Eugene Carroll also tried to dismiss any concern about Fort Drum by means of an exaggerated analogy:

We're training one division [of light infantry] in Alaska. Tell me which Eskimo tribe we are going to invade.[658]

He here sets up the Inuit as an example of insignificant, powerless people whom it would be contemptible to attack. He does not even

[656] D. Gore (1988) "Canada Needs to Bolster World Military Role: Brig. General," *Queen's Journal*, Sept. 30, p. 3.
[657] J.D. Salant (1991) "The War that Never Was," *Post-Standard* (Syracuse), March 25, p. A4.
[658] J. Picton (1991) "Is US Base Potential Threat to Canada?" *Toronto Star*, Dec. 1, p. A7.

know that they do not come in "tribes." By equating Canada with this image of Inuit, he makes clear what he thinks of Canada.

A rather complex analogy was put forth by Lieutenant-Colonel Rick Williams, one of the staff officers at Kingston Forces Base: to say that Fort Drum's lack of a rationale implies that it is there to threaten Canada is like "saying that all the events taking place in Eastern Europe at the moment are as a result of the Canadian government's [1987] decision to recreate the First [Canadian] Division."[659] Apparently this analogy argues that because it is silly to think that a Canadian force-structure decision could have any consequences, it is silly to think that a US force-structure decision could have any consequences.

Finally, it should be recalled that US President Harding ridiculed historic Canadian concerns about Manifest Destiny by saying that US designs on Canada are like Canadian designs on the United States. Because it is silly for Canada to try to conquer the United States, it is silly to worry about the United States planning to conquer Canada. Two Canadian strategic planning experts, Alex Morrison, director of the Canadian Institute of Strategic Studies and Len Johnson, former director of Canada's National Defence College, have tried to use the same analogy for the same effect. Speaking about *War Plan Red* and the potential threat of Fort Drum, Morrison said:

In fact, during the 1920s and 1930s Canada had its own plans to invade the US. That scheme, part of regular defence planning, called for the seizure of areas along the Great Lakes, part of Maine, as well as the cities of Spokane, Seattle, Albany, and Minneapolis.[660]

Johnson wrote:

Somebody down there no doubt heard about Colonel "Buster" Brown and his 1920s *Defence Plan Number One*, recalled the defeats of American forces in

---

[659] D. Hogan (1990) "Too Close for Comfort? Military Experts Divided on Theory Fort Drum May be a Threat to Canada," *Whig-Standard*, March 24, p. 4.

[660] D. Pugliese (1990) "The Americans are Coming! The Americans are Coming!" *Ottawa Citizen*, Dec. 30, p. A1.

1775 and 1812-13, and sensibly decided not to tempt the fierce Canadians with the prospect of easy pickings.[661]

Indeed, Sutherland-Brown has long been ridiculed for his *Defence Plan Number One*.[662] But it is a misconstrual to say that he planned to "seize" US cities, or that *Defence Plan Number One* is equivalent to *War Plan Red*. Mockery here displays ignorance. Brown's plan called for rapidly mobilized, mixed forces to penetrate as deeply as possible into the United States in order to effect a destructive retreat so as to forestall a US invasion long enough for the British to come to the rescue. Brown's contemporary detractors were unaware of *War Plan Red*, as it would seem are those Canadian military experts who still ridicule him. However, a former US deputy undersecretary of the Army who has studied *Defence Plan Number One* in historical context, finds little cause for mockery:

Fanciful, maybe, given the relative strengths of the two combatants. But who is to say that the desperate dash of Buster Brown's 'Flying Columns' in all-out defense of their homeland would not have bought the precious days necessary for British reinforcements to reach the scene — especially since the authors of Joint Plan RED seem not to have envisaged such aggressive action by the Canadians?[663]

TOO MANY EXPLANATIONS

What must not be missed in this great variety of explanations, excuses, and ridicule about Fort Drum is the very fact that there is such a plethora and such a variety. Individual critics may give many different explanations and some ridicule to boot, seeming to hope that something will hit the mark. Nobody has been able to say with persuasive confidence why the United States is situating these new

[661] Major-General (retired) L.V. Johnson (1990) "Don't Tempt Canadians" (letter), *Whig-Standard*, April 14, p. 8.
[662] C. Taylor (1977) *Six Journeys: A Canadian Pattern*, Toronto: Anansi.
M. Starowicz (1974) "Epilogue: The Great Unfinished Task of Col. J. Sutherland Brown," in R. Chodos and R. Murphy (eds.), *Let Us Prey* (pp. 181-197), Toronto: James Lorimer and Company.
R.A. Preston (1974) "Buster Brown was not Alone: American Plans for the Invasion of Canada, 1919-1939," *Canadian Defence Quarterly*, vol. 3 (no. 4), pp. 47-58.
[663] T. Holt (1988). "Joint Plan Red," *MHQ: The Quarterly Journal of Military History*, vol. 1 (no. 1), p. 55.

kinds of military forces at this period of history at the point Fort Drum occupies on the Canadian border. Americans and Canadians alike, lay public and experts, all have to guess and surmise.

Great effort seems directed to defending the belief that the United States simply would not use military force against Canadians. Americans need this belief in order to retain their own self-regard as trustworthy rather than treacherous. Canadians need this belief because they would otherwise be unbearably defenceless before US military might. No matter what facts come forward, people strive doggedly to defend these beliefs, with arguments if possible, with ridicule if necessary.

The United States has numerous military facilities near the Canadian border, from Loring Air Force Base in Maine to the Great Lakes Naval Training Center in Michigan, to the nuclear missile silos in North Dakota, to the Bangor Naval Base for Trident nuclear submarines on the West Coast. All of these facilities have had believable military rationale. There is little doubt that they were well-situated for their missions or that they could perform those missions. No one raised questions about whether or not these bases were directed against Canada.

If someone had, they would have been ignored. There would have been no response. There would have been no discussion and no ridicule. There would have been no guessing what the missions were, under what conditions they would go, whether or not the bases could perform those missions. The rationale for most of these bases has been credible. With Fort Drum, however, there is nothing credible. There are only questions and suspicions.

CHAPTER 12

CITIZENS' DEFENCE IN DEPTH

If the concerns expressed thus far about Fort Drum and other US military preparations are valid, it is not clear what can or should be done. Perhaps diplomatic efforts should be initiated to reduce or change the configuration of forces at Fort Drum. Perhaps conventional defences should be restored in Eastern Ontario. Perhaps a "Swiss" defence of well-trained militia should be organized. Militia were the mainstay of Canadian defence in the nineteenth century.[664] However, traditional reactions to military threat seem unlikely to be successful. They might even be counter-productive, since they institutionalize, structure and thus legitimize a posture of opposition between the United States and Canada. They allow traditional belligerent behavior patterns to follow well established courses.

In 1976, in a special journal issue commemorating the 200th anniversary of US independence, Canadian political theorist Hume Wrong articulated the difficulties of Canadian defence:

---

[664] R.A. Preston (1977) *The Defence of the Undefended Border: Planning for War in North America 1867-1939*, Montreal: McGill-Queen's University Press.

No sane military judge would decide that Canada could oppose the United States by force of arms or that it would make sense to precipitate a confrontation, but some civilians might be ready to fight as a last resort. It cannot be denied that if American leadership again reaches the low moral and intellectual standards of the Nixon regime, all forecasts based on previous experience may prove wrong. Furthermore, the rigid sense of patriotic duty indoctrinated in American officers, which marked their conduct during the Vietnam War, might open the way for them to be used as tools of unscrupulous politicians or resource-hungry corporations. Another possibility is that instability in a Canadian province that chose to secede from Confederation might bring covert or overt interference if it seemed to endanger the United States ... The Canadian-American relationship assumes a degree of responsibility on the part of Canada and a degree of restraint on the part of the United States that makes it unlikely that a critical point will be reached. But Canadian nationalists fear that exercise of moderation may inevitably mean the eventual demise of Canada.[665]

Thus, the traditional military responses to threat do not seem to be viable options. But that does not mean that Canada need continue in the passive angst articulated by Wrong.

Rather, Canada might actively pursue the objective of "defence in depth" using civil means. Sutherland-Brown advocated that Canada must seek defence in depth, which he interpreted as geographic depth achieved by the military seizure of territory.[666] Hence, he planned to attack into the United States in order to get space for retreat. Geographic depth would have created temporal depth: the need was to secure time. Time allows foreign nations to come to Canada's assistance. Time allows US political and popular opposition to war the opportunity to organize and become effective. In 1972, Mark Starowicz reviewed Sutherland-Brown's defence plan and prepared a modern equivalent. His unorthodox plan called for

---

[665] H. Wrong (1976) "Two Centuries in the Shadow of the Behemoth: The Effect on the Canadian Psyche," *International Journal*, vol. 31 (no. 3), pp. 413-433, quoting from pp. 430-431.

[666] C. Taylor (1977) *Six Journeys: A Canadian Pattern*, Toronto: Anansi.

R.A. Preston (1974) "Buster Brown was not Alone: American Plans for the Invasion of Canada, 1919-1939," *Canadian Defence Quarterly*, vol. 3 (no. 4), pp. 47-58.

M. Starowicz (1974) "Epilogue: The Great Unfinished Task of Col. J. Sutherland Brown," in R. Chodos and R. Murphy (eds.), *Let Us Prey* (pp. 181-197), Toronto: James Lorimer and Company.

Canadian forces to seize and hold hostage critical Canadian resource and industrial centres and transportation systems.[667] This is essentially a strategy of gaining defensive depth by threatening to destroy the prizes of conquest, thus making the aggressor pause and take heed. However, defence in depth need not always be sought and achieved by military force. It also might be achieved through Canadian civilian actions and US political actions. That will be the focus of these closing comments.

CIVILIAN NONVIOLENT DEFENCE

Canada's most cited theorist on peace and security is Anatol Rapoport from the University of Toronto. Looking only at macro-geographic considerations, he concludes that the United States is the only realistic military threat to Canada:

If we look at Canada's so called "defence needs" soberly, that is, with the jaundiced eye of "realism," as the defence establishment is supposed to look at those needs, we are forced to the conclusion that Canada has only one potential "enemy," namely, our neighbor to the south. From no other source is it in the least realistic to expect an invasion of Canadian territory, if only because the logistics of such an invasion would be totally unfeasible. In contrast, an invasion by the US would be logistically possible and under certain circumstances perhaps sufficiently motivated.[668]

Professor Rapoport went on to argue that there is no possible conventional military defence against an American invasion:

... the only chance Canadians would have in protecting their independence would be some form of nonviolent resistance, based essentially on strictly disciplined total refusal to cooperate with invaders or obey their orders.

George Crowell of the University of Windsor similarly argued before the Citizens' Inquiry into Peace and Security that Canada adopt civilian-based defence.[669]

---

[667] Ibid.
[668] A. Rapoport (1990) "The Three Branches of the Peace Movement: Research, Education, Activism," *Peace* (Toronto), vol. 6 (no. 5), pp. 16-18, quoting from p. 18.
[669] L. Priest (1991) "Civilian-Based Defence Best, Inquiry Told," *Toronto Star*, Oct. 8, p. A11.

National defence based on passive resistance, civil disobedience, and economic sabotage has had an effectiveness that is not well appreciated. It successfully stymied the Nazi occupation of Denmark during World War II. It defeated British rule on the Indian subcontinent after the War. It deserves more credit than all of NATO's military might for defeating the Soviet occupation of Eastern Europe. And these successes were based on the actions of a minority of people organised after foreign occupation had occurred.

Gene Sharp of Harvard University has been arguing that civilian nonviolent defence would be much more effective if the whole population were involved and if it were organised before a military power had taken control.[670] Moreover, it would produce a powerful deterrent effect if any would-be aggressor knew that occupation would be costly and that no economic benefits would be forthcoming. Gandhi claimed that nonviolent defence is most effective against nations with democratic ideals, like Great Britain and the United States.[671] The advantages of civilian nonviolent defence are that it does not threaten one's neighbours, it is very inexpensive and it displays trust between a people and their government. Lithuania, a small country with limited resources facing the overwhelming military might of Russia, is basing national defence on organized and coordinated nonviolent resistance by the entire population.[672]

---

[670] G. Sharp (1985) *Making Europe Unconquerable: The Potential of Civilian-Based Deterrence and Defense*, Cambridge, Mass.: Ballinger.

[671] V.T. Patil (1988) *Mahatma Gandhi and the Civil Disobedience Movement*, Delhi: Renaissance Publishing House.

[672] S. Kinzer (1991) "Lithuania's New Defense Minister Young Man with a Nonviolent Strategy," *New York Times*, Sept. 4, p. A12.

    R. Appressyan (1992) "Defending Lithuania Nonviolently," *Ploughshares Monitor*, vol. 3, March, pp. 1-4.

EXPOSURE AND INQUIRY

Appealing and practical as it may be, civilian nonviolent strategic defence is probably too new a concept for one to reasonably expect it to be implemented in Canada. Furthermore, Canada may now lack the political unity, leadership and trust necessary for such a scheme. Another strategy is to seek defence in depth, through US public opinion and politics. There is a need to effectively lobby the US public and its Congressional representatives to restrain, restrict and begin to direct US military planning. Foreign policy should be a civilian, not a military prerogative. Now that the United States has no overt enemy, why must it continue covert military planning? Secrets now are only secrets from US citizens and their democratically elected representatives.

A necessary first step in restoring civilian control is to expose covert US military planning against Canada and any US manipulations of Canadian political development. Such information would encourage public inquiry and public response. Canada's best defence is an informed, effective and commanding democracy in the United States. Preston concludes his history of secret US military preparations against Canada: "The future independence of Canada may continue to rest ultimately on American forbearance."[673] Forbearance requires both public foreknowledge of US military planning and public goodwill towards Canada.

The neighbours to the south of Canada have high ideals and a high national self-image. It is true that these very ideals and self-image may blind the nation to the reality of its actions and are too often paraded as justifications for foreign military interventions. However, despite evidence of failings and coverups, despite argument that those very ideals have been manipulated to hypocritical ends, the United States has shown a remarkable readiness to call to account

---

[673] R.A. Preston (1977) *The Defence of the Undefended Border: Planning for War in North America 1867-1939*, Montreal: McGill-Queen's University Press, p. 233.

those in power who violate those ideals. Would the Watergate or Iran-Contra investigations — insufficient as they may prove to be — have occurred in Britain, Germany, Japan, or even Canada? Probably not.

Canada is held in high esteem in the United States.[674] Canada represents the "kinder, gentler" society many Americans seek for themselves. Most US citizens, politicians, and military people would repudiate plans to attack Canada. They would be outraged if US agencies had been covertly designing Canada's disintegration. Canadians should appeal to the values and goodwill of the American people and their representatives. Canadians should more actively cultivate their own US constituency. Canadians should encourage and aid those politicians and citizens' groups in the United States that seek to regain control of their military planners and foreign policy conspirators. US political and popular interest and action require that there first be information. The light of inquiry — illumination — is what is now needed.

It is not in Canadian interests to ignore the activities at Fort Drum or to remain silent about these concerns. There is a fact that Canada must face. A foreign nation, one with a history of continental expansion against which Canada has historically had to defend itself, has made an unprecedented and unusual deployment of rapid reaction assault forces on the Canadian border. This gives them the permanent capability, whether by prior intention or not, of quickly assaulting Canada and splitting the nation at any time deemed necessary, day or night, summer or winter.

---

[674] M. Hogben. (1992) "Canada through Other Eyes," *Whig-Standard Magazine*, May 16, pp. 7-9.

ABOUT THE AUTHOR

It is natural, maybe inevitable, that Floyd Rudmin would expose US militarization of the Canadian border. Straddling boundaries and crossing borders has been a major feature of his life. He was a middle child in a family of six. His sister, Lynn, also a middle child, is herself politically active on progressive issues of community safety and social justice. Maybe middle children develop antennae for abuses of power, unfairness and fraud.

A public school valedictorian, Floyd studied philosophy at Bowdoin College in Maine. Two years in the US Peace Corps in the Philippines followed by two years teaching in Japan sharpened a critical eye to US policies and military power.

With language studies in Latin, Spanish, Chinese, Filipino, Japanese and French, his career moved to applied linguistics at the University of Buffalo and cross-cultural psychology at Queen's University in Kingston. Dr. Rudmin holds a joint appointment in Law and Business at Queen's University. He has over 100 publications on topics of ownership, history, peace and communication disorders.

With his wife, Toyoko, he moved to Canada in 1978. They have three children, Katrina, Christopher and Daniel.